SAN FRANCISCO PERFORMING ARTS LIBRARY & MUSEUM SERIES, NO. 4

THE SAN FRANCISCO STAGE

Part II:

FROM GOLDEN SPIKE TO GREAT EARTHQUAKE, 1869–1906

By MISHA BERSON

SAN FRANCISCO PERFORMING ARTS LIBRARY & MUSEUM SERIES
No. 4
FEBRUARY 1992

SERIES EDITOR:	STEPHEN COBBETT STEINBERG
EDITOR:	DAVID GERE
EDITORIAL ASSISTANT:	LENA STRAYHORN
DESIGN DIRECTOR:	CAL ANDERSON
COMPOSITION:	MARK WOODWORTH
PRINTING:	ALANS, INC.

The SERIES is published irregularly by the San Francisco Performing Arts Library & Museum (SF PALM). The price is $15 (domestic) and $20 (foreign). The SERIES continues the Library's former publication, the SF PALM JOURNAL. Back issues and prices available on request.

Address all correspondence to: Publications,
SF PALM, 399 Grove Street, San Francisco, CA 94102.

San Francisco Performing Arts Library & Museum Series

ISSN 1060-6858   ISBN 1-881106-03-9

COVER: SARAH BERNHARDT IN VICTOR HUGO'S *HERNANI*

INSIDE COVERS: THE GRAND OPERA HOUSE (ALSO KNOWN AS WADE'S OPERA HOUSE), CIRCA 1876

Contents

Preface 6

1. The San Francisco Stage: Act II 9
2. Excess & Quality: The Silver Era 15
3. David Belasco: A San Francisco Apprenticeship 27
4. 'The Passion': Spectacle & Scandal 35
5. From the 'Lily of Love' to the 'Divine Sarah': Stars Rush In 41
6. The Tivoli: A Home for Light Opera 55
7. Hiss the Villain, Cheer the Girl: The Age of Melodrama 63
8. Slummers' Paradise: Joints, Dives & Variety Halls 71
9. 'Genuine Negroes': African Americans Take the Stage 79
10. The Ol' Orph: San Francisco Embraces Vaudeville 91
11. Entertainment Alfresco: The Lure of the Open Air 101
12. Fairy Queens, Chorines & Free Spirits: Women Change the Dance 109
13. Earthquake Eve on the Town: April 17, 1906 133

Photography Credits & Notes 141
Index 144
About the San Francisco Performing Arts Library & Museum 148

BERT WILLIAMS, VAUDEVILLE STAR

Dedication

"The soul of Adonais, like a star,
Beacons from the abode where the Eternal are."
Percy Bysshe Shelley, *Adonais*

This book is lovingly dedicated
to the late Stephen Cobbett Steinberg,
whose intelligence, erudition, and passion
for San Francisco cultural history
guided me in all I have written here.

Preface

This book is the second in a three-part monograph series tracing the theatrical history of one of the world's most fascinating and idiosyncratic cities. After finishing the first volume, which covered the Gold Rush years (*The San Francisco Stage: From Gold Rush to Golden Spike*), I thought I had reached the end of the truly flamboyant era of the city's stage life.

In a sense I was right: Get past the Gold Rush and you lose some of the reckless individualism epitomized by characters like Lola Montez, Stephen Massett, and Adah Isaacs Menken, entertainers who came to the city when it was ramshackle, remote, and prone to flashfire enthusiasms. I was delighted to discover, however, that in the next phase of San Francisco theater there was no dearth of vibrant, willful personalities to consider. And the many new factors to take into account—accelerating technology, the birth of a nationwide show business circuit, and the changing demographics and tastes of the San Francisco region—added new layers to my research. I discovered that, while San Francisco did indeed lose something in its headlong rush toward progress and urban development in the years 1869 to 1906, it also retained its sense of bravado, the spirited vanity and gumption that persist to this day.

I have concentrated here, as in the earlier volume, more on cultural trends and influential individuals than on descriptions of architecture and listings of productions. In the interest of brevity, I have also chosen not to revisit genres that I covered earlier. For example, white minstrelsy and Chinese theater continued in San Francisco during the period traced here, but they are dealt with in far more detail in the previous monograph.

I also want to note that a promised bibliography of books related to San Francisco theater and a chronology of important events will be included in the third volume of this series. That final monograph will cover

SAN FRANCISCO PANORAMA, 1888

the period from the Great Earthquake to contemporary times.

Most of my research for this book was conducted at the San Francisco Performing Arts Library and Museum (SF PALM), and all but three of the accompanying photos are from SF PALM's excellent collection. I also found helpful resource materials at UC Berkeley's Bancroft Library, the San Francisco Public Library, San Francisco State University Library, and the Drama Library at the University of Washington, Seattle.

My heartfelt thanks go to David Gere, who stepped in at the eleventh hour to take over the editing of this project. He was a godsend. I also want to thank Margaret Norton, Lena Strayhorn, and the rest of SF PALM's unfailingly helpful staff, as well as Cal Anderson, Mark Woodworth, Barry Witham, Ann Daly, and my compassionate mate, Paul Schiavo. Without the enthusiasm of Tom Layton, and the financial assistance of the Wallace Alexander Gerbode Foundation, Zellerbach Family Fund, Columbia Foundation, Fleishhacker Foundation, California Council for the Promotion of History, and Firemen's Fund Foundation, this project would not have been possible.

I also need to acknowledge several people whose solid historical research gave me a foundation to build on: Lois Rather Foster and her colleagues on the multivolume San Francisco theater history study conducted by the Works Progress Administration in the 1930s, Russell Hartley (the late founder of SF PALM), Robert Toll, Walter Courtney Krumm, and John Scott McElhaney.

Finally, there is my deep and abiding gratitude to the late Stephen Cobbett Steinberg, who helped me conceive the *San Francisco Stage* series and worked very closely with me on nearly every phase of it as long as he was able. He was a true friend and collaborator, and I miss him very much.

Seattle, January 1992

Misha Berson is a longtime San Francisco arts journalist and educator who currently teaches in the School of Drama at the University of Washington, Seattle. For ten years she was principal theater critic for the San Francisco Bay Guardian, *and her work has also appeared in the* Seattle Times, Los Angeles Times, San Francisco Chronicle, American Theatre Magazine, The Drama Review, *and many other publications. In addition to SF PALM's San Francisco Stage monographs, her book credits include* Between Worlds: Contemporary Asian American Plays *(Theatre Communications Group) and essays in the new* Cambridge Guide to American Theater *(Cambridge University Press).*

The San Francisco Stage:
Act II

On May 10, 1869, before a small crowd of observers at Promontory Point, Utah, the rails of the newly constructed Central Pacific Railroad were officially joined to those of the Union Pacific Railroad.

San Francisco eagerly awaited word of this marriage of steel to steel. When news of it reached the city by telegraph, municipal offices shut down for the day, magnums of champagne were uncorked, people cavorted in the streets, and a gaggle of drunken revelers paraded down Montgomery Street with a banner that read, "San Francisco Annexes the United States!"

Act II of the San Francisco drama had begun, ushered in with characteristic bravado by an expectant citizenry. And although the completion of the transcontinental railway did not bring the unbridled prosperity some promised (actually, it brought on a depression), its economic, social, racial, and cultural impact on San Francisco would be profound and lasting. The next year freight and passenger trains would leave Boston and arrive two weeks later on the opposite coast. The first cross-country rail travel wasn't so easy (the trip was later reduced to three days), but it was a far cry from the arduous, months-long overland and sea journeys (via Panama) that brought travelers to California during the Gold Rush era.

First proposed in the 1850s, the railroad took a decade of political maneuvers and six years of hard labor by roughly 15,000 workmen—many of them Chinese—to complete. But San Francisco had not postponed growing up until this transcontinental artery was built. In the two decades between John Sutter's 1848 discovery of gold in the Sierra and the Promontory Point ceremony, the city's population swelled from 800 to nearly 150,000, the fastest growth for any major American city up to that time. [1] By 1869, the community was leaving its pioneer days in the dust and hurtling toward urban maturity at phenomenal speed—so quickly, in fact, that it was hard for outside observers to keep up with the changes.

In the 1870s and 1880s, visitors were often startled to find that San Francisco was no rough-and-ready pioneer outpost, but a burgeoning metropolis with paved roads, gas street lamps, a frenetic stock exchange, elegant hotels and restaurants, first-rate theaters, gabled mansions for a

"[San Francisco] is full of excess, singularities and contradictions. Since the discovery of gold it has abounded in sensations, financial, political and social. . . . It has been and still is, American in the extreme, and extravagant, therefore, in everything. It has all the intensity of youth . . . and although it is generous to prodigality, enterprising to rashness, hospitable to satiety, hopeful to visionariness, it has naturally lacked steadiness."

Boston Herald, quoted in the *Argonaut* January 14, 1882

9

DOWNTOWN SAN FRANCISCO IN THE 1890S

Despite concerted anti-Chinese political campaigns in the late 1800s and legislation restricting new immigration from China, San Francisco's Chinese theaters endured. A Chinese opera performer (below) *strikes a pose in typically elaborate costume. Lotta's Fountain* (opposite), *located at Market and Kearny streets, was a gift to the city from Lotta Crabtree, the famous actress who got her start in Gold Rush San Francisco.*

platoon of millionaires, middle-class enclaves of distinctive Victorian houses—as well as slums, unemployment, smog from unregulated coal burning, political corruption, and racial conflicts. This was no longer an outpost of transient single men; women were gaining in numbers and would reach near-parity with males by the turn of the century. Families had multiplied, more churches and schools dotted the landscape. The city had even instituted its own ingenious mass transit system: fleets of hill-climbing cable cars, the attractive conveyances introduced by Andrew Hallidie that would become emblems of San Francisco.

Visiting the city in 1882, New York journalist W. H. Bishop registered surprise at its sophistication: "San Francisco should be a vast motley camp. It should exhibit only a combination of squalor and mushroom splendor. The hovel should elbow the tawdry palace, a democratic boorishness of manners prevail, vulgarians blaze in diamonds, and the few refined natures that by chance have ventured into the midst shrink abashed to the wall. . . . [However,] camp it is none, but a solid, luxurious city."[2]

In the last quarter of the nineteenth century, the pace of urban "progress" would accelerate sharply in California and throughout the United States, eliminating much of the regional individuality of American municipalities. Such was the case for San Francisco, which grew more ordered and conventional the larger it got—particularly when compared to what it was like in its chaotic infancy.

But the city also clung stubbornly to certain aspects of its exuberant Gold Rush personality. The open hedonism and pursuit of instant wealth continued; so did tolerance for eccentricity and mass appreciation of flamboyance. Though a late-1870s campaign of racist demagoguery by Denis Kearney and his Workingman's Party succeeded in driving out part of the city's sizable Chinese population, San Francisco remained a multiethnic fusion of Asian, Hispanic, and European cultures. It was also still a magnet for gamblers, men willing to stake everything they had on the next big silver strike, the next pyramid stock market scheme, the next hot land deal. And, through the end of the century and beyond, the city continued to indulge in blatant self-congratulation and self-promotion—while constantly looking to New York, Boston, London, and Paris for approval.

Most significantly for our purposes, San Francisco did not surrender its tremendous passion for theatrical entertainment—a passion that dated back to the days when it was a slapdash frontier village full of bachelors on the prowl. Amusements of all sorts were in demand then, and pioneer theater producers such as Thomas Maguire, Catherine Sinclair, and E. G. "Doc" Robinson rushed to provide them, as did family acting troupes like the Chapmans and the Starks. Before the town had decent streets or adequate food supplies, it had performances of circus troupes and Chinese operas; Shakespearean tragedies and knockabout minstrel shows; plays in French, Italian, and German; ballet extravaganzas and operas—a variety and profusion of stage diversions few American cities could match.

More than seventy theaters came and went in the 1850s and 1860s, many lost to the periodic fires that ripped through the young city. Plucky international celebrities (Lola Montez, Edmund Kean, Adah Isaacs Menken) swept into town for lucrative engagements, while budding stars (Edwin Booth, Lotta Crabtree, Matilda Heron) polished their talents on local stages.

With many highs and lows along the way, San Francisco's theaters continued to be the primary source of public diversion between 1870 and the calamitous Great Earthquake of 1906. But the character of entertainment was transformed constantly in response to the changing times. Thanks to the transcontinental railroad, show business went national, and San Francisco became the major hub for dance, drama, opera, and vaudeville troupes on a West Coast tour circuit that eventually extended from Seattle to Los Angeles. Due to shifting patterns of local commerce, the city's "legit" stage activity migrated south from Portsmouth Square (the first municipal center), to the new, more fashionable downtown area around Market Street. Local trains and ferries began bringing in theater patrons from the outlying towns of San Jose, Oakland, and Santa Clara, and those communities also started to erect some playhouses of their own.

The great technological inventions of the late nineteenth century also had an impact on theater. Electricity altered the look of lighting and other aspects of stagecraft. The overland telegraph and streamlined photographic processes changed the nature of publicity, increasing the flow of information and flood of hype surrounding national and international celebrities.

Press coverage of performers and live performance was at a zenith during this time. In the 1880s there were over one hundred periodicals published in San Francisco, and the stage action was covered by many of them. Reviews appeared in journals of opinion like the *Wasp*, the *Argonaut*, and *Figaro;* literary magazines such as *Les Jeunes* and *The Lark;* foreign language organs like the *Courier de San Francisco;* and daily

newspapers including the *Evening Bulletin,* the *Post,* the *Morning Call,* and two increasingly dominant gazettes: the *San Francisco Chronicle* (which by 1875 had a circulation of 40,000 per day) and *San Francisco Examiner* (commandeered by brash young William Randolph Hearst).

The era saw a growing specialization among arts critics and the new practice of signed notices—a break from the old San Francisco custom of critical anonymity. In the mid-1880s the *American Dramatic Directory* named twenty-two staff drama and music critics on San Francisco publications.[3] Among the best known were Peter Robertson (the *Chronicle's* longtime drama critic), the *Call's* opera reviewer Blanche Partington, *Examiner* theater correspondent Ashton Stevens, the brilliant but bilious Ambrose Bierce (who, at various junctures, wrote for the *Argonaut,* the *Examiner,* the *News Letter,* and *Wasp*), and the *Argonaut's* chatty theater scribe, Betsy B. Not that readers slavishly followed their advice. As Samuel Williams noted, "San Franciscans are remorseless arbiters. They pride themselves on their ability to form independent judgements, and on their contempt for the opinions of the rest of mankind."[4]

A further sign of San Francisco's hopping commercial theater activity was the appearance of a local "trade" newspaper, the *San Francisco Dramatic Review.* This *Variety*-style tabloid lasted from 1899 to 1908, catering primarily to the throngs of professional performers based in the city or passing through in touring companies. Its pages carried large photo portraits of beautiful young actresses, ads for elocution coaches and stage make-up, puffy reviews of plays and concerts, and columns of theatrical news from correspondents in Spokane, Honolulu, Fresno, Portland, New York, and other cities.

Shifting social factors had a very potent effect on theater. In the Gold Rush days, San Francisco had been an exceptionally democratic place: Virtually everyone in town was a newcomer and a stranger, fortunes could be made and lost in a twinkling, and class distinctions were blurred by shared rustic conditions and boomtown camaraderie. In the 1850s, miners and gents rubbed elbows at the theater without complaint—and the gun battles that occurred during some performances involved both the highborn and the humble. But as the city grew and its wealth was consolidated in the hands of a select few, lines were drawn and San Francisco's social order hardened. The rich dressed up in ostentatious jewels and finery. They enjoyed preshow suppers of fresh oysters and champagne at the Old Poodle

Dog, the Maison Dorre, and other swank eateries. And they ensconced themselves in the boxes and orchestra seats of the grander auditoriums. The less well-heeled (and, usually, the non-Caucasian) were relegated by price, racism, and plain snobbery to "cheap seats" in the balcony.

Cultural tastes also grew more class-bound. Shakespeare and grand opera, once accessible to all, became the province of the intelligentsia and the social elite. Variety shows and lurid melodramas were devised specifically for working class viewers. And the fast-growing ranks of the middle class leaned toward vaudeville, operettas, and the more genteel manifestations of melodrama. Some viewers "crossed over," of course. But, more and more, producers were divvying up the market and targeting their wares to a specific social stratum.

During the years evoked here, San Francisco theater (like San Francisco in general) was rushing pell-mell into a new century, barely pausing to catch its breath or take its bearings. An astute young English reporter observed during an 1889 visit that the city was "a captivating rush and whirl" of frenzied activity. "Recklessness is in the air," wrote the not-yet-famous Rudyard Kipling. "I can't explain where it comes from, but there it is. The roaring winds off the Pacific make you drunk to begin with. The excessive luxury on all sides helps out the intoxication, and you spin forever 'down the ringing groves of change . . .' as long as money lasts."[5]

In the end, the money didn't run out, but the seismic stability did. After San Francisco had been flattened by the 1906 earthquake and rebuilt from the ground up, nothing would ever be quite the same. This, then, is a portrait of a culture in motion—at a time when live performance still dominated the public imagination and San Francisco was still the undisputed, incorrigible queen of West Coast cities.

The Columbia Theater (originally Stockwell's Theater) and the New California Theater were leading playhouses in turn-of-the-century San Francisco. A typical offering at the Columbia, which was controlled by the all-powerful New York–based Theatrical Syndicate, was Florodora *(above left), a fluffy Broadway-London musical sensation that hit San Francisco in 1901. The California went through several changes of management before it was torn down in 1888. In 1883, under Haverly's watch, it featured the historical melodrama* Francesca da Rimini *(above right), based on incidents from Dante's* Inferno.

Excess & Quality:
The Silver Era

Boom and bust, bust and boom—San Francisco's economy had zigzagged between the two since the first hurrah of the California Gold Rush. In the 1870s the city's fortunes fluctuated even more wildly between prosperity and disaster, and the theater business mirrored those fluctuations.

The decade began with a decisive boom, thanks to an outpouring of silver from the Comstock Lode and other Nevada mines, a frenzy of speculation at the California Stock Exchange (formed in 1872), and high hopes for rail-driven transcontinental commerce. Ironically, all these factors would contribute to San Francisco's worst economic crash yet. But the bonanza also yielded a crop of multimillionaires more opulent in their tastes, and more influential to the city, than even the Gold Rush nabobs.

In a story titled "Much Dinero," the *Morning Call* of August 6, 1871, reported that 122 San Franciscans controlled $146 million of the city's wealth. The richest was railroad tycoon Leland Stanford, with a personal fortune of $10 million—roughly equivalent to $250 million today. Stanford, fellow "Big Four" railroad baron Mark Hopkins, silver speculator James Flood, and other well-heeled citizens were flaunting their affluence by building the city's first genuinely ostentatious mansions. (The Hopkins castle on Nob Hill cost $3 million and had a hundred turrets in its glorified gingerbread design.)

Tastes in entertainment grew more extravagant too. Among the social elite, "first nighting" at the theater in diamonds and furs was *de rigueur*. But the older, slightly shabby theaters near Portsmouth Square, like the once-elegant Metropolitan, simply would not do anymore. As the locus of public life shifted south toward Market Street, larger and more ornate culture palaces would follow. Escalating civic pretentions and the growing desire for luxury and spectacle demanded it.

The era brought San Francisco three extremely grand new venues: the California Theater, Baldwin's Theater, and Wade's Opera House. The largest and best-equipped auditoriums in town, they swiftly became the most artistically significant venues the city had yet known and the mainstays of the dazzling (if short-lived) Silver Era of theater. Fittingly, two were

"With the 1870's, San Francisco entered upon its Arabian Nights era of sultanic palaces, fantastic towers, gold dinner services, silver balustrades and doorknobs, Oriental carpets, Chinese brocades, marble, brass, glass, lutes, flutes, trumpets and kettle-drums, marquetry, parquetry, Pompeian frescoes, South African diamonds, rainbow apparel, extravagance and extravaganzas. The Silver Era far surpassed the Golden Days of Forty-nine in spectacular incident and display. The river of silver streamed over the city and engulfed it."

Julia Cooley Altrocchi
The Spectacular San Franciscans
1949

"Frisco is blessed with an overabundance of theaters, opera houses and halls, and as they all have sufficient money to start with and not enough to end with, it is not at all astonishing that we find the city full of idle artists, actors, variety people of all grades, ready and willing to do job work at reasonable figures, or even hand round the hat."

New York Dramatic News
February 3, 1877

WILLIAM C. RALSTON, DRESSED FOR
A MASQUERADE PARTY

Two portraits from the California Theater's glory days: Adelaide Neilson, a favorite visiting star, played Juliet to Mrs. Judah's Nurse in an 1874 production of Romeo and Juliet *(above).* Emelie Melville *(opposite), a featured actress at the California, was described by the* Dramatic Chronicle *in 1868 as a young woman "with bright blue eyes that sparkle like diamonds in the merry moods, and melt into a world of tenderness in the pathetic passages."*

bankrolled by prominent local tycoons, the other by a moneyed dentist making his bid for top-shelf respectability.

William C. Ralston made his great imprint on local culture by building the spacious, elegant California Theater in 1869. Brash and self-assured, a theater-lover and masquerade ball aficionado, Billy Ralston had a well-earned reputation as one of the West's flashiest self-made millionaires. His story, tangled up with the California Theater's, epitomizes the era's wild excesses, its sudden swings of fortune and misfortune.

Ralston settled in San Francisco in 1853 at the tail end of the Gold Rush and quickly rose from steamship agent to chief financial officer of the powerful Bank of California. Thanks to his shrewd machinations, the bank became a major player in the Silver Rush and helped engineer the speculation spree that followed.

Described by native San Francisco novelist Gertrude Atherton as "a thick-set man with a massive face" whose blue eyes were "piercing but kind and often humorous," the affable Ralston had the cash and the imagination to dream expansively.[1] Convinced that California should have the biggest and best of everything, he poured money into risky start-up industries—sheep ranches and irrigation projects, furniture and machinery factories. He spent extravagantly in his private life too, maintaining a fabulous villa in Belmont and throwing elegant balls at his San Francisco townhouse.

When it came to constructing the California Theater, he didn't pinch pennies. The plush new playhouse was erected on fashionable Bush Street, near Kearny Street, at a cost of $150,000. Ralston put up $50,000 from his own pocket, and also paid out the sums needed to keep up the theater's lavish style of production.[2] (Before his mysterious death in 1875, Ralston would spend far larger sums on his own Xanadu: the fabled Palace Hotel.)

Ralston footed the bills at the California Theater, but artistic matters were left completely to its esteemed manager, John McCullough. For a year with fellow actor-manager Lawrence Barrett, then for eight more years on his own, the ruggedly handsome, well-liked "Genial John" upheld a sterling quality of production at the California, leaving a bench mark for resident San Francisco drama that has perhaps never been surpassed. McCullough also introduced important innovations of stagecraft to the West Coast—including the first box set (a realistic set with ceiling and walls) in 1877. Many agreed with company member Walter Leman, a veteran character actor, when he wrote that the California "was for nine years the best managed and most prosperous theater in the Union, the best theaters in New York, or any other city, not excepted."[3]

Cast most effectively as a "heroic" actor in meaty Shakespearean roles, McCullough had been a protégé of the great tragedian Edwin Forrest. He continued to perform in many California Theater productions but also engaged the services of the nation's other great leading players—including his former partner Lawrence Barrett, Edwin Booth, John Brougham, Charlotte Thompson, Adelaide Neilson (a charismatic young actress on whom Billy Ralston had a flaming crush), and the playwright-actor Dion Boucicault (author of the wildly successful plays *London Assurance* and *Rip Van Winkle*). McCullough embellished these stars with top-flight sets (usually designed by the California's brilliant resident scenic artist, W. T. Porter), and with supporting actors of the highest caliber.

In fact, the California elevated San Francisco's theatrical reputation by boasting one of the country's last great "stock" companies. In the nineteenth-century stock system, before national touring outfits replaced most regional ensembles, theaters would give actors long-term contracts to portray specific "types." Employment broke down into standard categories: the Leading Man and Leading Lady (for shows with no imported star), the Light Comedian (young lovers and juvenile roles), the Heavy (villains and middle-aged men), the Walking Gentleman (anything from bit parts to leads), the Soubrette (attractive young women who broke into song), and so on.[4] The continuity of the company allowed the actors to work as a unit in show after show, resulting in the kind of seamless ensemble playing found in the best British repertory troupes.

The California's hand-picked crew of fifteen actors and nine female actresses included the cream of San Francisco's talent pool, as well as noted veterans from the New York stage (where hard economic times had made theater employment scarce). Emelie Melville, Marie Gordon, John Raymond, Harry Edwards, and beloved Gold Rush character actress Mrs. Judah were a few of the California players who became not only public favorites but respected members of the community—no mean feat, considering the shaky social status of performers in those years.

But these actors really earned their respect, and their pay. During its first year alone, the California Theater presented some three hundred performances. (The theater was dark only on Sundays, by law.) To keep

audiences coming back, the theater's managers changed bills frequently and usually offered a full-length drama plus a light one-act. In their first year on the boards, the California company performed twenty-five dramas, five full-length comedies, and several dozen short curtain-closers—which meant the actors had to memorize and rehearse roughly seventy different scripts! During this period, McCullough alone essayed twenty-seven different roles, including such major assignments as Romeo and Iago.[5]

At first the California emphasized high-toned fare: Shakespeare's ever-popular *Macbeth* and *Richard III,* historical dramas like Adrien de Mauprat's *Richelieu,* and literate British comedies such as Sheridan's *The Rivals.* But McCullough soon learned that the San Francisco audience demanded change and splashy novelties—especially in the form of "leg" dramas and blow-out musical extravaganzas.

In 1870 a *News Letter* critic sounded the warning bell. "I am a constant visitor of the California Theater, and lately have seen with sorrow the gradual but sure falling away both in number and style of the audiences that filled the dress circle and orchestra," he wrote. "What Californians must have, is variety. We want new faces."[6]

McCullough took the cue and expanded his repertoire, thereby engaging in cutthroat competition with producer Tom Maguire. Maguire, as everyone in town knew, could be a formidable rival. A Forty-niner, he had been San Francisco's first successful entertainment impresario, a trailblazer who supplied the city with world-class drama when it was still a raw, lawless mud hole.

Though no longer the all-powerful "Napoleon of the San Francisco stage" he had been in the 1850s, Maguire was far from retired in the 1870s. He still wheeled and dealed frenetically, presenting hit-and-miss seasons of minstrel shows, circuses, and musical spectaculars at Maguire's Opera House, the Metropolitan Theater, and other venues.

Those extravaganzas, featuring scantily dressed (for the times) female troupes like Lydia Thompson's British Blondes, really packed 'em in—and they were the wave of the future. By the winter of 1869, McCullough beat Maguire at his own game by producing a lavish, pseudo-Shakespearean "fairy spectacle" called *Cherry and Fair Star.* It had all the crowd-pleasing ingredients of the genre: a brood of dancing fairies in form-fitting tights, a picturesque woodland setting, such froufrou props as a chariot trimmed in peacock feathers, and even an onstage shipwreck. Plus it had

Fanny Davenport was among the many commanding leading ladies to appear in the city during its star-struck period. Signed on by the famous producer Augustin Daly for his first road company, she later used her business acumen to produce her own tours. Critic William Winter described her in 1879 as a "voluptuous beauty, radiant with youth and health . . . and [with] a voice as naturally musical and cheery as the fresh incessant rippling flow of a summer brook."

the California's imprimatur of quality. Writing in the *News Letter*, the tough critic and acerbic social observer Ambrose Bierce judged it "the best of its kind that we have had on this coast."[7]

McCullough continued to wage box office war with Maguire by staging other overblown fairytales, like *Sinbad the Sailor* and *Paris, or The Apple of Discord.* (The latter, according to the *Daily Dramatic Chronicle*, featured plenty of "symmetrically proportioned" limbs "encased in flesh-colored silk tights" and illuminated "by the reflected brilliancy of hundreds of flaming gas jets.")[8] At one point the producers squared off with simultaneous,

Cast primarily in meaty "heroic" roles, Irish-born actor John McCullough was a ruggedly handsome Shakespearean veteran who became a much-respected manager of the California Theater. He hired the best actors available, brought in the most lustrous stars, and gilded them all with excellent sets and costumes. When forced by Billy Ralston's death and financial circumstances to surrender the California in 1877, McCullough went back on the road as a touring performer. In 1884 he had a mental breakdown during a performance in Chicago and died the next year, at the age of fifty-three.

competing burlesques of San Francisco's favorite opera, *La Sonnambula*.

Despite its increasingly commercial fare, the California did not, however, give itself over entirely to frivolity. Excellent stock players and classical headliners kept up the playhouse's reputation for serious drama. Apart from top-notch editions of the classics, McCullough also brought the city its first look at the new sensations of London and New York: *Pygmalion and Galatea* by W. S. Gilbert, *Saratoga* by Bronson Howard, and Augustin Daly's blockbuster melodrama *Under the Gaslight*. Increasingly, cosmopolitan San Franciscans were looking toward the East Coast and Europe for theatrical crazes. They craved the latest "certifiable" sensations in their own theaters, even if they got them a year or two later.

Dramas by the first wave of serious West Coast dramatists also debuted at the California—with mixed success, given mercurial popular tastes and the fact that American playwrighting still lagged behind what England and the Continent had to offer. One of the most tenacious San Francisco playwrights was Clay M. Greene. In 1871 his critically praised *Love* failed miserably, while the crowd-pleasing novelty *Ready! or California in '71* by Fred Lyster and W. H. Sedley Smith hit big—thanks mainly to the gorgeous painted backdrops of Seal Rock, the Golden Gate, and Yosemite. Later Greene fared better with *M'Liss*, a rough-and-ready frontier tale based on a Bret Harte story. And in 1874 the California presented a dramatization of Greene's *The Gilded Age*, a tale written by Harte's old Gold Rush pal Mark Twain. (Twain immediately disowned Greene's version and adapted the story himself for a New York theater.)

Billy Ralston justifiably took great pride in the California Theater and was seen in its best box on many an opening night. As the silver strikes continued, he kept on subsidizing the California's costly operations. And in 1874 he began planning for a much more extravagant brainstorm, the Palace Hotel. Ralston's $6 million spending spree on the Palace has been recorded by San Francisco historian Oscar Lewis in all its amazing detail. The seven-story, 800-room hotel would be the largest building erected in the West up to then, quickly becoming *the* hostelry for visiting theatrical stars, tycoons, presidents, and European royalty. Occupying a full block on Market Street, it would boast all the latest advances—indoor "water closets" and gas fixtures, electric lobby clocks, artesian wells, and its own fire-fighting squad (which, unfortunately, didn't help much in the 1906 fire). The furnishings were custom-made, the fine china and crystal imported. But surely the most striking feature was its 84-by-100-foot central court, a series of seven white balcony-style galleries rising up to a roof of domed glass that suggested a massive white wedding cake.[9]

But Ralston himself would not be present at the Palace Hotel's gala 1876 opening. In 1874, silver stocks began to falter after an orgy of speculation and backstage manipulations by Ralston and rival financiers. The situation quickly went from bad to disastrous, and on August 26, 1875, there was a run on funds at the Bank of California. Ralston sold off many of his own assets to raise capital, but he was already overextended and couldn't stave off the panic. Closing the bank early that day, he set off alone for his daily swim and drowned in the frigid waters of San Francisco Bay. Perhaps it was suicide, perhaps he got caught in treacherous cross-currents. To this day his death at the age of forty-nine remains a mystery.

Ralston's sudden demise and the calamity of the Bank of California crash cast a pall over San Francisco, raising major questions about the silver mania. Many agreed with the *News Letter*'s assertion that Ralston had been "a prince" who "greatly aided and assisted in building up this city."[10] Others remembered him as a "reckless" financial gambler involved in "the wildest and most dangerous stock speculations."[11] The same could be said of many other San Francisco speculators—but none of them had died so strangely, nor left behind such a financial tangle.

The California Theater was, of course, hit hard by this turn of events. Ralston had made up deficits and even floated large personal loans to McCullough, who meanwhile managed to regroup and keep control of the California until 1877. But a general depression, fueled by the end of the Silver Rush and the failure of the railroads to bring instant prosperity, loomed on the horizon. Even before it struck, other forces would undermine the California's position—including the 1876 construction of Wade's Opera House and Baldwin's Academy of Music.

The fact that two giant new theaters opened in such tense economic times was an illustration of San Francisco's relentless optimism about its fortunes. Actually, Wade's Opera House (at Mission and Third streets) had been in the works for some time. Erected by a group of investors headed by local dentist Dr. Thomas Wade, the massive Italian Romanesque structure had seats for 2,500 spectators. Decorated in various shades of blue, the luxurious auditorium boasted elaborate chandeliers that ran on electricity (a rarity at the time), a stage 85 feet deep by 106 feet wide, and a drop

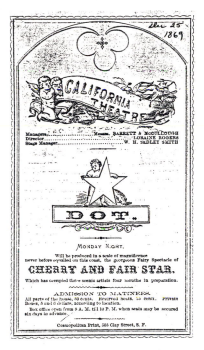

curtain described by the *Chronicle* as "a tropical scene, with water, islands, palms and flowers, and a group of naiads disporting in the foreground." All told, the initial construction and equipment costs amounted to $750,000.[12]

Wade's opened on January 17, 1876, under the eager management of Frederick Bert with a "ballet extravaganza" called *Snowflake*—an early entry in a long line of form-over-substance musicals that paved the way to *Cats* and *Phantom of the Opera.* The January 18 *Alta California* pronounced this *Snow White* knock-off "a pretty, though somewhat tedious fairy story, in five acts . . . [with] beautiful scenery, a host of songs, a magnificent ballet, and beautiful transformations." Audience members, however, were just as impressed by the sheer scale of the theater. As writer B. E. Lloyd so benignly put it, "Upon entering, the immense size of the auditorium is at once remarked."[13]

It may have been blue inside, but Wade's Opera House was soon known around town as a white elephant. Keeping this behemoth running turned out to be a great challenge for the many who tried. The lease changed hands and the building changed ownership several times before its demise in the 1906 earthquake. The name changed too, from Wade's Opera House to Morosco's Opera House and then simply to the Grand Opera House.

The nature of the stage attractions changed more often than the name. One can even look at the Opera House as a three-decade barometer of local theatrical fads. Lush burlesques and spectacles drew the biggest crowds in the 1870s, along with such crowd-pleasing slices of Americana as the plays *Rip Van Winkle* and *Buffalo Bill.* In the 1880s under Walter Morosco, grand-scale melodramas reigned, while in the 1890s superthespians like Sarah Bernhardt, Henry Irving, and Ellen Terry made their local debuts on the spacious stage.

By the turn of the century grand opera took over, with music-lovers turning out to welcome Emma Abbott, Nellie Melba, Enrico Caruso, Sibyl Sanderson, and other singing stars of the era. But Chinese operas, vaudeville revues, and "rural dramas" (like *Davy Crockett* and *Way Down East*) were also featured at various junctures—in short, whatever would fill the immense hall in a rapidly changing show-business economy.

Meanwhile, on March 6, 1876, less than two months after Wade's gala opening, the Baldwin's Academy of Music entered the scene—managed by that tireless old theater hand Tom Maguire. Baldwin's Academy was part of

From 1876 to 1906, the Grand Opera House, on the north side of Mission Street between Third and Fourth streets, was San Francisco's largest and most opulent playhouse, a home for grand opera, touring super-thespians, spectacular action melo-dramas, splashy musicals—in short, anything that might fill 2,500 seats. Many managers took a turn running this gaudy behemoth, and it remained in operation until the 1906 earthquake tumbled it down.

22

The Baldwin Theater was part of the elegant, six-story Baldwin Hotel owned by E. J. "Lucky" Baldwin, a wealthy hotelier and high-rolling gambler. From its glittering opening in 1876 to lean times in 1882, the Baldwin was managed by that tireless old theater hand Thomas Maguire. Later it came under control of the Theatrical Syndicate, which brought such stars as Julia Marlowe, Helena Modjeska, and the young romantic actor Otis Skinner to play for the Baldwin's always-fashionable audiences.

a huge hotel complex owned by Elias Jackson "Lucky" Baldwin, yet another Comstock Lode potentate. Like Billy Ralston, Baldwin thrived on venture capitalism and reveled in an imperial standard of living. But, apropos his nickname, he was graced with better fortune.

Judging from eyewitness reports, Baldwin's 1,969-seat theater was even posher than Wade's Opera House. Socialite Amelia R. Neville remembered its "red plush upholstery, velvet hangings, gilt scrolls, and filigree work in the decorations, which gave it precisely the effect the gay rich San Francisco of its day approved."[14]

The Baldwin opener, *Richard III*, starring the famous Irish actor Barry Sullivan, was first and foremost a brilliant social event. And for a while Maguire kept the stars right on coming. He also installed a stock company that he hoped would outshine the one at the California.

He failed in that. But for the next two years, both he and McCullough did provide the city with a bounty of great acting. Frederick G. Ross, a player who worked at the California, remembered the two stock companies as "friendly rivals. Actors of both houses were pretty busy at all times, but did occasionally fraternize together. Once in a while, it might be that when a serious scene was being given at one or the other theater, right in the middle of it, the leading man of the opposition theater . . . would suddenly walk right on in this scene and at once proceed to improvise talk of a kind. The audience loved these little episodes."[15]

With three opulent auditoriums competing for top attractions and public favor, the San Francisco theater business was very complicated indeed in the 1870s. Wade's, Baldwin's, and the California had a collective seating capacity of over 5,000, in a city whose population was growing rapidly but still under 250,000 in 1880. And the big three weren't the only theaters in town—Maguire's Opera House, the New Alhambra Theater, and others also vied for public patronage.

By 1877 the silver output had diminished and the financial climate was deteriorating. Bank failures multiplied, unemployment skyrocketed, and even the San Francisco *nouveaux riches* that heavily patronized the theaters felt the economic pinch. Desperate measures were taken to keep the major theaters from going under. As his California Theater company crumbled, McCullough tried his hand at running the Baldwin, and Maguire took a turn running Wade's Opera House. But in the end, as attendance waned, many fine actors were forced to exit the city and seek work elsewhere. In 1877 even the dedicated McCullough regretfully left town.

The *San Francisco Chronicle* summed it up this way: "The decline of theatrical interest in the city . . . is the result of many causes, chief of which we take to be the new era of thought and feeling that followed the suspension of the Bank of California. . . . San Francisco never really had a death in the family until Ralston's, and until the recent past no great financial trouble. So we have lived on hopefully and buoyantly, with an exuberant life, a continual overflow of feeling, a gush of sentiment, and the abounding good nature that comes from all these conditions, ready always to seek the fullest measure of enjoyment for all genuine sources of amusement. We have given theaters a fulsome and often over-indulgent patronage. From it all has come an excellent knowledge of dramatic matters and development of a critical instinct to be hereafter more shrewdly exercised."[16]

For the next few years theatrical patronage ground to a near-halt in the city. Some producers, including Tom Maguire, tried to tough out the bad times. But the expensive California stock company was a casualty of depression; when it disbanded, it was like the dissolution of one of San Francisco's favorite families. Though several managers would run the California Theater before it was demolished in 1888 (to be replaced by the less important New California), none would come close to matching McCullough's level of accomplishment. Nor did "Genial John" repeat his achievement elsewhere. Resuming work as a touring actor, he eventually suffered a mental breakdown, was confined to a hospital for a time, and died in 1885 at the age of fifty-three.

In retrospect, the 1870s were undoubtedly a halcyon period for the San Francisco stage. Amidst all the greed and ostentation, the speculation and shortsightedness, the expansive frontier city procured "the fullest measure of enjoyment" from drama—and, with the railroad in operation, eagerly began to draw on the wealth of top-rated talent that it had been denied during the catch-as-catch-can 1850s and 1860s.

Imported talent would increase exponentially by the end of the century. But even as it did, the city would retain its penchant for discovering, encouraging, and grooming dynamic young theater artists—a custom that began in the Gold Rush era and persists today. As researcher Walter Krumm has noted, "If nothing else the San Francisco stage of the [1870s] was a drama school *par excellence*."[17] One of its most eager pupils was a future Broadway titan named David Belasco.

Building the grand Palace Hotel was one of the extravagances that led Billy Ralston into financial ruin. The interior court is pictured here as it was in 1890. The seven-story, 800-room hotel was the largest building erected in the West up to that time, quickly becoming the preferred hostelry for visiting theatrical stars, tycoons, presidents, and European royalty.

25

David Belasco:
A San Francisco Apprenticeship

In 1871, when San Francisco's Lincoln Grammar School held its annual elocution contest, there was little doubt who would pocket the gold medal in the "Tragedy" category.

Seventeen-year-old David Belasco—"Dave" to his pals—made an indelible impression on the judges with his recitation of "The Maniac," an emotive poem by Matthew Gregory Lewis. Actually, the word recitation doesn't do justice to Belasco's performance. Writhing on the floor of the school stage, his hands bound in chains and his face streaked with dirt, he impersonated a madman with such vocal and physical ferocity that a teacher thought the boy "would one day break a blood vessel."[1]

By that time, Belasco's flair for the dramatic was no secret to his elders and peers. The stagestruck teenager had already snagged bit parts and walk-ons at Maguire's Opera House and the Metropolitan Theater. He had organized an amateur drama club. He had even written and directed plays of his own—starting, at age twelve, with *The Roll of the Drum,* a drama set in the aftermath of President Abraham Lincoln's assassination.

No one knew it yet, but this small, dark, exuberant youth was on his way to a spectacular Broadway career as one of America's first great theatrical *auteurs:* a producer, playwright, scenic wizard, starmaker, theater owner, and master of staging determined to control all facets of his art. Belasco's innovative use of hyper-realistic lighting, sets, costumes, and acting, coupled with his middle-brow taste for flagrantly romantic love stories, brought him enormous wealth and fame. A prolific creator, he put the "Belasco touch" on nearly four hundred productions and became the dominant American theatrical figure of his epoch. Most of his melodramatic plays have not endured the test of time, but Belasco did have lasting impact as a scenarist and as one of the first of a new breed of visionary showmen to expand the role of "director."

Before Belasco came into his own on Broadway, he served a colorful, action-packed apprenticeship on the California stage—as his idols Lotta Crabtree and Edwin Booth had done a generation before. During much of his California period, Belasco lived the life of a journeyman actor and all-

"One cannot begin to dream too soon if one expects to transform the dream into reality, and I believe that most men who have accomplished anything have had the dream in early boyhood."

Interview with David Belasco
New York Times
January 31, 1904

DAVID BELASCO IN *UNCLE TOM'S CABIN,* CIRCA 1878

STAGE STAR ADELAIDE NEILSON

ACTOR-MANAGER JOHN McCULLOUGH

around stagehand—unsung and scrambling. For an inside view of San Francisco's silver-plated theater epoch, one need only consider his early career. He worked in scores of productions, soaked up many theatrical styles, observed the finest actors of his era, wrote his first scripts. And he received invaluable on-the-job training from producer Thomas Maguire, who took Belasco under his wing as he had so many other talented novices.

Years later Belasco conjured up the early California of his memory (and fantasies) in such sentimental plays as *Rose of the Rancho* and *Girl of the Golden West*. And in his published reminiscences he recalled his own West Coast youth with great fondness—while liberally embellishing the facts of his life with fictions.

More dispassionate sources record that Belasco was born in San Francisco on July 25, 1853 (not, as he claimed, in 1859), to English immigrants of Portuguese-Jewish extraction. His father, Humphrey Belasco, had been a stage harlequin in Britain but in California turned to shop-keeping. In 1858, during a statewide economic slump, the elder Belasco moved his family to Fort Victoria, British Columbia, where a new gold rush was underway.

In a 1914 memoir written for *Hearst's Magazine,* Belasco described his boyhood as a string of romantic escapades involving Indian braves, sailors, kindly old priests, and precocious feats of artistry. He traced his adult habit of wearing a clerical collar (an affectation that earned him the nickname "the Bishop of Broadway") to a long stint in a monastery. And he described running off with a Brazilian circus to become a bareback rider—"Davido, the Boy Wonder!"[2]

Given that Belasco's parents were Orthodox Jews and that no record exists of any South American circus playing Fort Victoria at the time, both claims are dubious. But Canada's Wild West atmosphere and a steady diet of dime adventure novels inflamed Belasco's imagination. He began to act, making an auspicious debut at age eleven at Victoria's Theater Royal in *Richard III*, alongside the great English tragedian Charles Kean.

The Belasco clan (which soon included three more sons, two of whom would also take to the stage) moved back to San Francisco in 1865. When the city's theater scene erupted a few years later, young Dave took full advantage of it. He studied elocution, haunted the playhouses and acting agents' offices, and in 1869 helped form the Firefly Social and Dramatic Club, inspired by matinee idol Lotta Crabtree's lead performance in her popular vehicle *Fire-Fly*. A dual role in *A Life's Revenge*, a Firefly Club melodrama, brought Belasco his first press review. According to a *Figaro* critic, the young man "displayed much power and was ably supported by other members of the company."[3]

Emboldened by the praise (and the gold elocution medal), Belasco quit school for the footloose, hand-to-mouth life of an aspiring thespian. Working at first as "Walter Kingsley" (young actors often took stage names to avoid future embarrassment), Belasco played character roles, bit parts, and walk-ons wherever he could get them. He appeared in dramas, minstrel shows, farces, and musicales at the Metropolitan, the California Theater, Maguire's New Theater, and many other San Francisco playhouses, and even blacked up to assume the lead in *Uncle Tom's Cabin*. He also toiled backstage—as prompter, script boy, and errand runner.

Most often young Belasco worked as a utility player with second-rate companies. But now and again he had a chance to observe the first rank of American stage actors at close range. Eagerly—and briefly—he waltzed with the luminous Adelaide Neilson in an 1874 *Romeo and Juliet* at the California Theater. Two years later he was a watchful extra in a stellar season at the California featuring Edwin Booth, Lawrence Barrett, and John McCullough. These were master classes he would never forget.

Among Belasco's own roles, his impersonation of a real-life character named Emperor Norton commanded the most attention. Since the Gold Rush, San Francisco had attracted many eccentrics and given them a wide berth. "Emperor" Joshua Norton styled himself as the aristocrat of oddballs. A ruined businessman who believed himself to be the Emperor of the United States, Norton dressed in ceremonial military uniforms studded with brass buttons, tooled around town on an outsized tricycle, and often issued royal edicts—including one abolishing the Democratic and Repub-lican parties. Emperor Norton was regarded as an amusing mascot, and his delusions were mostly indulged. San Franciscans fed and clothed him gratis and encouraged his uniformed presence at such upscale social affairs as the grand opening of the California Theater. Even England's Queen Victoria and the Emperor of Japan responded graciously when he wrote them on "official" business.[4]

Like all San Francisco celebrities of note, Norton was often spoofed in the theater, beginning with the satirical 1861 operetta *Norton the First* at Tucker's Academy of Music. Belasco's turn to mimic him came in *The Gold*

POPULAR PLAYWRIGHT DION BOUCICAULT

EMPEROR NORTON, ECCENTRIC

Demon, one of the final offerings at the Metropolitan Theater before its demolition. The 1873 burlesque starred Ella and Blanche Chapman, descendants of the famous Gold Rush acting dynasty. Belasco took the minor role of Prince Saucilita, but everyone knew who he was impersonating in his whiskers and mock-military outfit. The *Figaro* again praised him by noting that "D. Belasco took the house by storm with his make-up for 'Emperor' Norton, which was quite a feature of the piece."[5]

When work grew scarce in the city, Belasco barnstormed up north with the hardy little troupes that still played the mining circuit. Later he recalled a typical rough-and-tumble tour with the Fulford Company: "I beat the drum and Annie blew the cornet upon entering a town. We played anywhere, sometimes in a tent or an earthen floor stage. . . . Always low in finances, we were forced to rent hotel rooms without advance payment; this was accomplished by presenting hotel managers with a locked tin strong box filled with stones, and asking them to watch our gold for us until we leave."[6]

Though Belasco scratched out a living on the road, he never succeeded as a performer. He wasn't tall enough or, ultimately, talented enough to land major parts. Throughout his San Francisco career, Belasco would resort to odd acting jobs and tours when he needed money. But at twenty-one he tagged up with several men who helped him discover where his real talents lay. Under their influence he would turn his prodigious energies to stage managing, writing, producing, and eventually directing.

One of Belasco's role models was the hugely popular Irish playwright-actor Dion Boucicault, whom he briefly assisted during a short tour in the Sierra. But others of more prolonged influence were the aging impresario Tom Maguire and James Herne, an actor, budding dramatist, and Maguire's trusted stage manager.

The association between Maguire, Herne, and Belasco proved especially fruitful, if erratic. It lasted off and on for eight years, encompassing some seventy-five flops and hits at various theaters. The three first worked together in 1874, when Belasco hired on as Herne's general backstage helper for one rocky season at Maguire's New Theater. Two years later, when Maguire opened the plush new Baldwin's Academy of Music, Herne and Belasco were his chief lieutenants—as they would be during Maguire's several go-rounds at the Baldwin.

Managing the Baldwin turned out to be Belasco's first big break and

Maguire's last hurrah. Ever the intense competitor, Maguire was determined to beat the highly respected California Theater at its game. He formed the rival Maguire's Unequalled Company and installed the charismatic young James O'Neill (later the father of playwright Eugene O'Neill) as principal leading man. (Little Maude Adams, a pretty child actor and future adult sensation, was also part of the ensemble when needed.) Stars were brought in on occasion from Broadway and Europe, including the British-

Ella Chapman was a member of San Francisco's most famous Gold Rush acting clan, the Chapmans. She and her sister, Blanche, hired David Belasco to impersonate "Emperor" Joshua Norton in their 1873 burlesque, The Gold Demon.

American favorite Rose Coghlan (who at first balked at having a "boy" Belasco's age as director), Joseph Jefferson, Lester Wallack, and Adelaide Neilson. The public was further courted with a constant supply of original and adapted dramas—many of them by David Belasco and James Herne.

These scripts had to be written and staged in an enormous rush. For example, four plays adapted by Belasco and starring James O'Neill—*Olivia, A Woman of the People, Proof Positive,* and *Not Guilty*—premiered at the Baldwin between September and December of 1879.[7] This pace was common in an era when American playwrights functioned more as script carpenters than literary creators. As Belasco later recalled, "A stock dramatist at that time was obliged to do his work on short notice, and it was taken as a matter of course that I should get a play ready for rehearsal in less than a week, and put it on in less than another week."[8]

Within these strictures, Belasco tended to write formulaic romances or cobble together his own versions of popular foreign dramas. Such practices got him into the habit of borrowing heavily (and in some cases stealing outrageously) from other authors, without always giving them due credit. With few copyright laws on the books, he generally got away with it. But charges of plagiarism would haunt him throughout his career. One of the first instances involved *Within an Inch of His Life,* a popular 1879 adaptation of Emile Gaboriau's novel *La Corde au Cou,* credited to Belasco and F. W. Lyster. Soon after the play opened at the Baldwin, a disgruntled Stephen Maybell fumed to the *San Francisco Call,* "Your humble servant, the undersigned, is the author of the piece, and the two gentlemen who would try and wear the reputation of another have scarcely even altered the original copy as it came from my hands."[9] A week later the *Call* printed Belasco's rejection of Maybell's claim and the incident blew over. But several years later Belasco and Herne's *Marriage by Moonlight* drew similar fire. It seems that this "new" play bore a striking resemblance to *Camilla's Husband* by Watts Phillips.[10]

Though Belasco displayed little originality as a writer while in San Francisco, he did develop a flair for staging plays far more vividly and inventively than the average stage manager of the day. In the early 1880s, theater was largely a matter of one-dimensional artifice. Sets were composed of flat, painted backdrops with rudimentary lighting, and the resulting environments looked anything but "real." Drawing on the new technology that would revolutionize stage lighting—and on his instinctive pull toward flamboyant naturalism—Belasco began to experiment with the multidimensional scenic effects and atmospheric nuances that would become his trademark.

Belasco's gift for special effects was first noted in reviews of a novelty show called *The Egyptian Mystery,* presented at the Egyptian Hall. By draping the stage with black velvet, placing the actors under a sheet of glass, and using concealed gas lamps as a light source, Belasco created what he later called "the impression of a phosphorescent light from ghostlike bodies."[11] The faithful *Figaro* commended his handiwork: "There can be no question about the fact that [these] are most extraordinary effects, however they may be produced, and the mingling of the ghostly and the real gives the queerest character to the performance that can be imagined."[12]

Later, at the more spacious Baldwin, Belasco could stretch out and direct in a sweeping, epic mode completely in sync with the growing demand for stage sensationalism. He turned Dion Boucicault's Old South romance *The Octoroon* into an expansive musical with a big cast that included the Callender's Minstrels. In his version of the Watts Phillips drama *Not Guilty,* he inserted a battle scene that featured a cast of hundreds, a real cannon, live horses, and a chorus singing music from Bizet's hot new opera *Carmen.* Theater-owner Lucky Baldwin was so impressed with this—and so convinced that Maguire was underpaying his protégé—that he gave Belasco a thousand-dollar bonus.

Belasco experimented with other innovations at the Baldwin. Inspired by the new naturalism in *L'Assoimoir,* Emile Zola's novel about the gritty underbelly of Paris, he injected lifelike effects into his adaptation of it. The *Evening Bulletin* critic described the show as "a picture of low life and of dissipated life . . . , fearfully realistic. . . . The nine tableaux are elaborate stage settings and the costumes of the numerous dramatis personae are as accurate as the dress of our own daily life could be presented."[13] A startling touch, according to the *Argonaut,* was a "wash-house scene where the contestants are drenched to the skin by full buckets of realistic wash-tub water."[14] In the same vein, the later Belasco-Herne drama *Chums* had a "finale with real rain falling on a line along the front of the stage."[15]

But the most ambitious and by far the most controversial San Francisco production Belasco collaborated on was *The Passion.* It was a piece of theater that had a powerful effect on the public and a profound impact on its key creators.

San Francisco loved Lotta Crabtree as a child variety performer, and it loved her as a grown-up gamine too. This publicity still shows the vivacious Lotta (also known as "The California Pet") in the late 1880s. In 1887 she gave her ardent fan David Belasco a thrill by appearing in a play he wrote with Clay Greene, called Pawn Ticket No. 210.

33

'The Passion':
Spectacle & Scandal

The Passion was one of the most astonishing theatrical productions ever conceived in San Francisco and one of the most spectacularly naive. The furor it aroused in the spring of 1879 prefigured flaps over the sacred and profane in art more than a century later, in works like Martin Scorsese's film *The Last Temptation of Christ* and Andres Serrano's photo *Piss Christ*.

The Passion was authored by Salmi Morse, a local newspaperman who, at the time, was editor of the *Wasp*, the popular San Francisco magazine. Morse, a Jewish man of intense disposition, claimed to have spent twenty years researching his American *Oberammergau*, and he was obsessed with seeing it produced. He brought the script to Tom Maguire and Lucky Baldwin along with a crumbling parchment covered with Chaldean, Arabic, and Roman symbols. Morse insisted that this arcane document authenticated his version of Christ's story.

Moved by Morse's script and manner—and ever on the lookout for novel spectacles—Maguire and Baldwin decided to give *The Passion* a lavish production at the Grand Opera House, a theater Maguire had run for brief intervals and the only stage in town big enough to contain a biblical epic. James O'Neill signed on to play Christ—a "role to which he considered himself peculiarly fitted," according to critic William Winter.[1] And who was better equipped to create the show's bold visual design than David Belasco? He conceived it as a series of richly-lit tableaux, peopled with a cast of four hundred men, women, and infants, plus droves of farm animals.

An air of ostentatious piety hung over the preparations for this strange production. O'Neill plunged into his role with great enthusiasm. The Irish-born actor was then thirty-two and the Baldwin company's prime matinee idol. O'Neill cut a dashing figure with his strong physique, jet-black hair and moustache, and flashing dark eyes, but he was eager to extend his artistic range beyond the one-dimensional male ingenue roles he often played. Acting Christ on the cross so inspired him that during the rehearsal period he abstained from the tobacco and alcohol he usually enjoyed, and purportedly spent hours alone in prayerful contemplation.

Belasco, meanwhile, took to carting around a Bible and studying the

*"I heard a voice out of Heaven
   crying—
I heard a voice from the earth
   replying.*

*FIRST VOICE:
"The Savior once was made to feel
Men's wrath at his behavior;
And now they lock up James O'Neill
For looking like a Savior.*

*SECOND VOICE:
"What on earth attests let Heaven
   record
Men's wrath at James they level
Because while looking like the Lord,
He's acting like the Devil!"*

An Editorial
Argonaut
April 19, 1879

35

JAMES O'NEILL AS JESUS IN *THE PASSION*

color effects in two large paintings at the Mercantile Library: one depicting the Dance of Salome, the other the Last Supper. To achieve his desired scenic effects, he also got busy rounding up every out-of-work actor, nursing mother, and barnyard animal in town.

The resulting panorama, from Belasco's glowing description, sounds nothing short of miraculous—a prototype for the cast-of-thousands biblical films made later by the likes of Cecil B. de Mille. "The play traced the whole sequence of historical events leading to the Crucifixion and Resurrection," Belasco later remembered. "In the Massacre of the Innocents we had a hundred mothers on the stage with their babies in their arms. In the scene where Joseph and Mary came down from the mountainside, we had a flock of real sheep following in their wake."[2]

Gaudiness was forsaken, Belasco insisted, for "a simplicity that amounted to grandeur. All was accomplished by fabrics and stage lighting, and when O'Neill came up from his dressing room and appeared on the stage with a halo about him, women sank to their knees and prayed, and when he was stripped and dragged before Pontius Pilate [who] crowned him [with] a crown of thorns, many fainted."[3]

Those were actually some of the milder reactions to the pageant. One faction of the audience—reportedly a small contingent of young Irish Catholic rowdies—became so enraged during the crucifixion scene that they rushed out of the theater to initiate a mini-pogrom. The spontaneous mob attacked anyone in the streets who looked Jewish and for good measure smashed up Jewish-owned pawnshops and other businesses.[4]

For their part, theater critics mostly damned the show on artistic grounds. The *Argonaut* reviewer called the play's dialogue "polysyllabic drivel." "That which to the Alpine peasant would be a spectacle of religious worship, filling his simple mind with pious ecstasy . . . ," he complained, "comes in these enlightened times to be but an absurd and irreverent money-making spectacle."[5]

But the loudest howls came from some incensed Protestant clergymen who deemed any stage dramatization of Christ's martyrdom sacrilegious—especially one written by a Jew. Before *The Passion*'s March 3, 1879, premiere, a number of ministers condemned the venture from their pulpits. The Reverend Dr. W. J. Smith was among the most vociferous. The Sunday before the show opened, he thundered, "I do not know of another city where they could put such a thing on the stage with impunity, unless it be

The Wasp, *an influential satirical journal, lampooned producer Tom Maguire in the cover cartoon of this 1881 issue* (below). *An 1884 handbill* (opposite) *advertised one of James O'Neill's many national tours in Alexander Dumas's* The Count of Monte Cristo, *a melodrama that enriched O'Neill's coffers but, on endless repetition, destroyed his talent.*

this God-forsaken city of San Francisco. . . . I pray that the lightning that played around the crest of Sinai may rend that stage from end to end."[6]

Less vengefully, but just as vehemently, Episcopal leader William Ingraham Kip wrote in the March 8 issue of the *Argonaut,* "No fearful impiety could be devised than such a presentation on the stage of a theater. We trust, therefore, that the feelings of our religious people will no more be outraged by making the scenes of Our Lord's Passion the objects of flippant criticism in this irreverent community."

Not all clergy agreed, and the Catholic leader of the region, Archbishop Joseph Sadoc Alemany, remained notably silent on the matter. But cries of outrage against the irreverence and moral laxity of San Francisco had been heard periodically since the Gold Rush and would crop up time and again throughout the city's history. For all its liberality and freewheeling tolerance, San Francisco has long harbored an arch-conservative minority poised to spring into action quickly, and often effectively, against alleged heathens and sinners. Despite appearances to the contrary, the puritan strain in American society did not bypass California; it just lay underground like a hidden fault prone to sudden, violent shocks.

The flap over *The Passion* would constitute the city's first major arts censorship battle. Despite their lukewarm reviews of the play, journalists squarely defended Maguire's right to produce it and made fun of the Reverend Smith and his ilk. But the city's Board of Supervisers knuckled under to the offended. They passed a remarkable municipal statute (Order #1493) which forbade "any person to exhibit, or take part in exhibiting, in any theater, or other place where money is charged for admission, any play or performance or representation displaying, or intended to display, the life or death of Jesus Christ, or any play, performance or representation calculated or tending to debase or degrade religion."[7] This law actually remained on the books until 1938, when it was finally repealed.

Fearing for his own safety after receiving death threats, Tom Maguire closed *The Passion* on March 13, 1879, after just eight performances. But to test the legality of the censorship measure and recoup part of his huge financial outlay, he brought the show back on April 15—right in time for Easter! James O'Neill, by now very much identified with the role of martyr, played Jesus once again.

As might be expected, the Opera House was packed to the rafters the

night *The Passion* reopened. The show progressed uneventfully, until just before the scene of Christ's removal from the cross. At this point, two San Francisco Police Department officers marched backstage and arrested O'Neill. The actor was led away wearing sandals, a flowing white robe, and a halo. Seven others associated with the play were also arrested.[8]

O'Neill vowed at first to fight the charges against him. In the end, however, he chose to plead guilty to a misdemeanor and pay a fine of fifty dollars; the others got off with five-dollar fines. On April 19 the *News Letter* acidly summed up the whole absurd but ominous incident: "It is not decorous England, or puritan Boston, that convicts Mr. O'Neill, nor is it some obscure, little village vestry board which might well be pardoned for narrow-mindedness. But in San Francisco—wicked, reckless, dashing San Francisco. . . . We expect next to hear of an ordinance for the burning of all old women who keep cats or have a mole on their noses."

The *Passion* debacle left its mark on all the principal collaborators. James O'Neill was crushed by the public hullabaloo and court case over what he considered his most fulfilling role—and what Belasco called "the performance of a generation." His ego and sense of piety wounded, O'Neill firmly believed himself "at the end of all success as an actor."[9]

But O'Neill's career was untainted; if anything, *The Passion* put his name on the lips of everyone in town. He went right back to playing boilerplate leading man parts at the Baldwin, then astonished all by deciding to revive *The Passion*—this time in New York. This plan brought about the end of the actor's eventful residency on the San Francisco stage, though he would return to the city later as Edmond Dantes in *The Count of Monte Cristo*—the romantic role that made him a wealthy man but turned him into a thespian hack. (He repeated it some six thousand times.)

Writer Salmi Morse took the failure of *The Passion* even more to heart than O'Neill. His play never did reopen in New York despite Morse's fervent hopes for its vindication there. In 1884 a producer agreed to back the venture, but before rehearsals could begin Morse was fished out of the Harlem River. No one knew for sure whether he had drowned accidentally or ended his melancholy life himself.

And Tom Maguire? *The Passion* was one of several big failures that finally bled the producer dry. The large deficit from the religious drama— added to Maguire's accumulated losses on grand opera, his inconsistent receipts at the Baldwin, and the still-deteriorating economy of San

In the 1870s James O'Neill cut a dashing figure as the handsome leading man of Maguire's Unequalled Company at the Baldwin Theater. At the time, the future father of playwright Eugene O'Neill had a strong physique, jet-black hair, and flashing dark eyes—attributes that led to his being typecast as the lover in standard romantic fare. But O'Neill longed to extend his range. For him, the role of Jesus Christ in Salmi Morse's The Passion *turned out to be a spiritual and artistic adventure—as well as an allegedly criminal act.*

Francisco—hastened the producer's financial demise. The aging impresario had managed a dozen theaters in his time, presented thousands of performances, been party to numerous acrimonious lawsuits, and exerted more influence on San Francisco's cultural development than any other individual. He had won big and lost big, but he had always bounced back. In April 1882 he ran out of bounce. Despite Belasco's steadfast loyalty, Maguire lost control of the Baldwin Theater and never managed a theater again.

Maguire stayed fitfully active in San Francisco show business until 1890. He then headed back to his native New York City and died there, penniless, in 1896. (His age was undocumented, but the newpapers guessed he was in his mid-seventies.) It was a sad ending for such a proud and accomplished man, but in his waning years perhaps Maguire took some comfort in noting the progress of Belasco and others he had helped.

Belasco remained loyally allied with the Baldwin until there was no hope of Maguire holding on to it. Then, in July 1882, he quit San Francisco to take a job as stage manager at Daniel Frohman's prominent Madison Square Theater in New York. Though rich in experience, he was just twenty-nine at the time, and his great theatrical triumphs—opulent productions of his plays *DuBarry, Zaza,* and *Madame Butterfly*—lay ahead of him. In later years he would return to the West Coast with his hit productions in tow and maintain close ties to his brothers Fred and Walter, who became successful San Francisco theater managers. But his future was Broadway, and a theater there still bears his name.

The saga of *The Passion* conjures a fading San Francisco stage epoch—a fluky, abundant, highly competitive drama scene prone to bold and extravagant gestures, ruled by artists and producers who made the city their home and had a real stake in its cultural life.

Increasingly, the swaggering independent producers like Maguire and the resident actor-managers like John McCullough would give way to a new brotherhood of cooler-headed, more calculating theater operators. These businessmen put profits before passions. They were attuned to national trends, hooked into Eastern theater syndicates, and more interested in San Francisco as a lucrative tour stop than as a dramatic wellspring. Although most didn't stay long in the city, they were the impresarios who ushered in its next major theatrical wave: the era of the combination tour and the star system.

During his four decades as San Francisco's reigning theater impresario, Tom Maguire managed a dozen theaters, presented thousands of opera and drama performances, launched the careers of many gifted young artists, and exerted more influence on the city's cultural development than any other individual. The failure of The Passion *hastened his loss of the Baldwin Theater in 1882 and forced his retirement soon after. Of their last days together at the Baldwin, David Belasco later recalled, "Although Maguire and I had our differences, I liked him, I pitied him, and I stuck to him till the end."*

From the 'Lily of Love' to the 'Divine Sarah': Stars Rush In

Lillie Langtry's first visit to San Francisco did not pass quietly. She swept into town with seven servants, thirty-two trunks, and twenty-eight valises in tow. When she opened at the Baldwin Theater on June 16, 1884, in *A Wife's Peril,* the "Lily of Love" (as her pal Oscar Wilde affectionately called her) was already renowned for her intimate friendship with Edward VII, Prince of Wales, and for her porcelain beauty. Only her abilities as an interpreter of dramatic literature remained in question.

In a full-page article printed on April 5, 1884, the *Argonaut* described Langtry's social escapades in detail and assessed her upcoming stage appearance as an opportunity "to test the question of how much talent and beauty it may require to make our fashionable and foolish forget themselves." Langtry passed the test at the box office: tickets for her debut sold out in an hour and sales for succeeding nights were brisk. But the fair-faced Englishwoman never did win high marks from local critics for her acting. One reviewer termed it "simply an excuse for permitting people to pay money to see her."[1] Nonetheless, Langtry generated enough public enthusiasm to return in style for engagements in 1884 and 1887. (In 1888 she also acquired a ranch in Lake County where she spent summers and tried her hand at winemaking and breeding thoroughbred horses.)

Lillie Langtry was one of many internationally-known stage performers to draw crowds in *fin de siècle* San Francisco. During an era that prized individual genius, many acting and operatic giants made their way west, Sarah Bernhardt, Adelina Patti, Henry Irving, and Nellie Melba among them. There were also leading ladies like Langtry and the New York socialite-actress Mrs. James Brown Potter, whose allure derived more from gossip and chic than talent. (They were famous for being famous.)

San Francisco's fascination with celebrity and flamboyance had been firmly established back in the Gold Rush days, when visits by famous stage folk to the remote West Coast were practically viewed as municipal holidays. Toward the close of the century, however, star turns grew almost routine. The grand celebrity tour was one of several trends that would radically—and permanently—change the nature of American entertain-

"In ten minutes an artist knows whether or not he is to be a success on the Pacific Coast. Success goes like an electric current through the audience, if it goes at all. If not, the audience remains quiet and shuts off the batteries. There is absolutely no recovery from a first night failure in San Francisco. The public is not merciless: it is indifferent. If an artist is a success in San Francisco, he is a great success, and there is magic in an enthusiastic San Francisco audience."

San Francisco Evening Bulletin
August 8, 1883

"The play is nothing—this, it would seem the managers would have us believe—it is the actress, her speeches, her scenes, her gowns, her personality that are the all-important essentials. It is notorious how plays are cut and readjusted and dislocated to suit the Star."

Frank Norris
Responsibilities of the Novelist
1903

41

LILLIE LANGTRY

ment. Thanks to the advent of the transcontinental railroad and some monopolistic business practices, the nation's theater was transformed from a patchwork of regional stock companies run by independent impresarios and actor-managers to a big business pushing standardized, star-studded "product" from coast to coast.

Celebrity-dominated show business would thrive throughout the country, but most emphatically in glamour-struck San Francisco. By 1882, the city was shaking off its post-silver economic doldrums and entering a period of prosperity that would last a solid ten years. In the booming late 1880s a record twenty-nine theaters were in operation, chief among them the four major "legit" houses—the Baldwin (which introduced electric stage lights in 1888), the New California (built in 1889 at Kearny and Dupont streets), the Grand Opera House, and an important 1885 addition, the Alcazar. There also existed four Chinese theaters and a wide assortment of smaller drama, music, and variety venues (among them the Bush Street Theater, the Tivoli, and the Bijou). According to census figures, San Francisco in 1890 boasted more theater seats per capita than any other major U.S. city—including New York.[2]

The outward expansion of the Bay Area helped to increase San Francisco theater attendance. As the neighboring towns of Oakland, San Jose, and San Mateo grew more populous, ferries and trains made scheduled runs carefully coordinated with theatrical curtain times. Shrinking prices also boosted ticket sales. In 1885, after some fierce price wars, one could buy a gallery perch at one of San Francisco's better playhouses for as little as ten cents and a top orchestra seat for roughly two dollars. (A superstar ticket could fetch four dollars, or much more if a scalper was doing the selling.)

And what kind of theater filled those seats? Mass tastes dictated a broad-based, populist aesthetic. Tear-jerking melodramas drawn from American life, rustic comedies, operatic extravaganzas, and rousing vaudeville shows became all the rage, largely supplanting the Shakespearean tragedies, Restoration comedies, even the minstrel shows of years past. "This is an era of horse play and ham fat," noted San Francisco's *Morning Call* on January 25, 1885. "And if the public want it, why of course . . . they shall have it."

Along with the hamfat and horseplay, the public wanted stars—and thanks to the expanding web of transcontinental rail lines, it got them.

An acclaimed Irish tragedian, Barry Sullivan starred in the memorable Richard III *that opened the Baldwin Theater in 1876. David Belasco played minor roles during Sullivan's engagement.*

Carting performers, costumes, and sets around by rail was, at first, an expensive and cumbersome undertaking. But the creation of booking circuits by men like San Francisco's Michael Leavitt made cross-country touring more efficient and (for wily producers) much more profitable. By the 1890s, several New York–based producers revolutionized touring by forming the Theatrical Syndicate (the "trust"), an all-powerful conglomerate that choked off most competition by controlling the nation's large playhouses, shaving costs of production, making sweet deals with the railroads, and shuttling scores of star-fronted companies from city to city on long, grueling tours. Al Hayman, who had managed playhouses in San Francisco, was one of the Syndicate founders and kingpins.

By far the most sophisticated and populous city west of the Rockies, San Francisco was the Pacific Coast jewel in the national touring crown. That status, however, did not always guarantee it first-rate road shows.

The "combination" touring system—the term used for star-led troupes that picked up supporting players along the way—ranked commercial concerns over artistic quality. Tours organized in the East might arrive in San Francisco one, two, even three years old and much the worse for wear. Too often, stars shared the stage with inferior colleagues—a sad contrast to the consistently fine acting of the great stock companies that offered superb training and consistent support. Frequently they appeared in creaky dramatic vehicles unworthy of their celebrated talents, or in decent scripts crudely altered to fit their public images.

Many leading performers hated the new system but felt helpless to change it. Minnie Maddern Fiske, a popular leading lady and frequent visitor to San Francisco, complained to the *Chronicle*, "The influence of the sordid and commercial control that seeks only the easiest method of securing the dollar and that has no aspiration and no conscience with respect to the advancement of American dramatic art, is nefarious. . . . The trust system naturally is the friend of mediocrity, and from mediocrity it can exact a large share of the profits."[3]

Whatever the touring system's pitfalls, it did bring a continual flow of the world's best-known performers to San Francisco, adding yet another coat of luster (if not much substance) to the city's reputation as a prime "show town." On the top rung of the ladder were the high-toned legitimate stars, considered the great thespians of the age: then-famous actresses such as Clara Morris, Kate Claxton, Mrs. D. P. Bowers, Fanny Davenport, Ada

Kate Claxton, a noted character actress, made frequent appearances on San Francisco stages. Some colleagues considered her a jinx because she had the misfortune to be playing in several theaters on the nights they burned down. But most critics were generous in extolling her charms, including one who found that Claxton excelled "in sweetness, in beauty, and in an innate refinement of manner."

OTIS SKINNER

MAURICE BARRYMORE

Rehan, Margaret Anglin, and male matinee idols like Frank Mayo (box office insurance in the lead role of *Davy Crockett*), Otis Skinner, young Maurice Barrymore (father of John, Ethel, and Lionel), Irish actor Barry Sullivan, and the suave Richard Mansfield.

Old favorites who had apprenticed on California stages and gone on to national success returned—though not always to rave reviews and full houses. James O'Neill, remembered by audiences from his Baldwin Theater days, revisited on many occasions but was soon chastised by critics for repeating his role in *The Count of Monte Cristo* ad infinitum. And though Shakespeare was no longer a populist favorite, America's great tragedian Edwin Booth managed to tour to San Francisco four times between 1887 and 1889—twice with Lawrence Barrett, another illustrious California almunus, in his company. On May 13, 1889, Booth and Barrett baptized the ornate New California Theater (under the management of future Broadway magnate Al Hayman) with their legendary production of *Othello*—followed by renderings of *The Merchant of Venice, Hamlet,* and *Julius Caesar.* The *News Letter* of May 11 praised Booth's opening as "one of the most brilliant society and dramatic events of California history."

But some critics were lukewarm about Booth's *Othello,* blaming the combination touring system more than the artist. Complained the *Chronicle,* "No man can be rushed around the country as if he were [in] one of the knockabout shows . . . and be as fresh as we want Mr. Booth to be, [or] as great as Mr. Booth can be."[4] Later this would seem a prophetic comment: Barrett's death in 1891 and Booth's two years later marked the close of America's golden age of classical acting.

Lotta Crabtree, a true daughter of the Golden West, was also a frequent return visitor to the city. In 1875 she presented San Francisco with an ornately carved outdoor drinking fountain that survived the 1906 earthquake and still stands on Market Street near Kearny. She last performed in San Francisco in 1891, the year she retired. Even then, at age forty-four, she seemed the eternal gamine in the musical comedy trifles *Musette* and *Ina.*

Many foreign stars also made their way west. They were often fussed over, but reactions from San Francisco's audiences and phalanx of critics could be extreme and unpredictable. A show's reception might be rapturously enthusiastic beyond an artist's wildest dreams or negative enough to discourage future visits.

When the famous classical Italian actor Tommaso Salvini played a three-week engagement at the Baldwin in 1886, critics swooned over his Othello, this despite the fact that Salvino played in Italian while his vastly inferior supporting cast spoke English. But Helena Modjeska, another European luminary who tried a bilingual gambit, initially got the cold shoulder from critics. Modjeska arrived in the U.S. in 1877, after fleeing Russian-occupied Poland with her husband, Count Charles Bozenta. She lived briefly on a communal farm in Anaheim with other Polish émigrés but soon accepted John McCullough's invitation to make her American debut in San Francisco at the California Theater. In May 1877 she delivered her first performance in English at the California, essaying the lead in *Adrienne Lecouvreur.* She followed up with an Ophelia in Polish—opposite McCullough's English-speaking Hamlet!

Despite her vaunted reputation, San Francisco critics trashed La Modjeska: "Few ladies have appeared on the San Francisco stage who have owed so much to womanly grace and sympathy and so little to distinguished talent," carped a *Chronicle* reviewer. He then went on to blast the audience for cheering the actress so heartily.[5]

But the audience prevailed. Thanks to her popular run at the California, Modjeska soon snagged a thousand-dollar-a-week touring contract. With a twenty-three member company managed by her husband, she crisscrossed the U.S. in a private, lavishly appointed rail car—a perk of stardom she patriotically christened the "Poland." When Modjeska finally returned to San Francisco in May 1883, local reviewers found more to praise in her quiet, unaffected style. The *Morning Call* gloried in her "graceful, swaying figure," her "pure and expressive face, the speaking eyes, the . . . limpid utterance."[6] She would enjoy other triumphant runs in the city before retiring in 1902.

Ellen Terry and Henry Irving, England's most celebrated Victorian acting team, made just one trip to San Francisco in the fall of 1893. (Their manager at the time happened to be Bram Stoker, the future author of *Dracula.*) During a two-week Grand Opera House run, Irving was harshly panned in the September 3, 1893, *Examiner* by a vitriolic Ambrose Bierce. Other reviewers alluded to Irving's tendency to overact, but Bierce went right for the jugular, concluding, "For German, English, and American actors we should provide 'homes' with light employment, good plain food, and, when they keep their mouths shut and their limbs quiet,

The celebrated Polish actress Helena Modjeska received a cool reception from San Francisco critics during her American debut at the California Theater in 1877. But audiences adored Modjeska, particularly in her signature role as Adrienne Lecouvreur, and she swiftly became a major touring draw throughout the nation. Otis Skinner, one of her leading men, was particularly impressed by La Modjeska's "eagerness and joy . . . a joy restrained and admirable in execution, the great joy of artistry."

45

thunders of artificial applause." But a *Bulletin* reviewer dissented, praising the actor's ability during a marathon fifteen-minute soliloquy in *The Bells* to "hold the audience by the sheer force of his high art."[7] Racking up ticket sales of $65,000, Terry and Irving managed to transcend Bierce's wrath.

Not all the stars who conquered San Francisco were so pedigreed as Irving and Terry. On another level entirely was Lillian Russell, a singer-actress known for her blond, busty looks, crackerjack comic timing, supple legs (she exposed them in naughty white tights), and cozy friendship with new York's colorful James B. "Diamond Jim" Brady.

Russell first hit San Francisco in 1881 with a troupe managed by early vaudeville impresario Tony Pastor and headlined by comedian Willie Edouin, an alumnus of the California Theater's stock company. But it was Russell who became the talk of the town. During her 1892 visit in the comic opera *La Cigale*, a reviewer gushed, "Lillian Russell is one of those very rare people who can even beat a lithograph." (She was prettier than her picture.) The enthusiastic critic went on to praise her "charming" singing and "emotional work that is sincere, earnest and genuine."[8]

San Francisco audiences also clamored for tickets whenever a visiting literary lion appeared onstage; Charles Dickens, Anthony Trollope, Walt Whitman, and Ralph Waldo Emerson were a few of the many writers who lectured at Platt's Hall. Back in 1866 a young newspaperman named Mark Twain accepted Tom Maguire's invitation to lecture at the Academy of Music, thus beginning a brilliant, lifelong speaking career.[9] In 1882 a very different man of letters drew much attention in town: Oscar Wilde, the famous Irish-born poet, playwright, and wit.

Wilde's excursion to San Francisco was part of a twenty-stop lecture tour to publicize the D'Oyly Carte Opera production of *Patience*—a Gilbert and Sullivan musical that humorously spoofed Wilde's aesthetic pretensions. As he traveled around California and the West, publicity followed the twenty-eight-year-old intellectual dandy wherever he went. Readers were curious about his theories of art, home decoration, and Irish poetry, but they were most fascinated by his unorthodox attire.

The first of Wilde's four San Francisco lectures was titled "The English Renaissance," and it was heard at Platt's Hall on March 27. Wilde did not disappoint those in the packed hall who were expecting sartorial splendor. He stepped to the podium dressed in a black velvet suit with

46

Lillian Russell, sex symbol of the Gay Nineties, was a star whose comic flair, way with a song, and buxom beauty kept her in the public eye—as did her dalliances with famous men and her four marriages. Her nickname, "Airy Fairy Lillian," gives a sense of the blithe, I-don't-care spirit she projected onstage and off. From her first local appearance with comedian Willie Edouin at the Standard Theater in 1881, San Francisco found her irresistible.

black silk knee breeches, patent-leather shoes with silver buckles, a white lace cravat, a cutaway coat with lace cuffs, and white kid gloves—a grown up version of Little Lord Fauntleroy.[10]

As a public speaker, Wilde proved disappointing. San Francisco reviewers complained about his nasal voice and monotonous delivery. And the splenetic Bierce took glee in savaging the content of his remarks. "Not

This well-known portrait of Oscar Wilde was taken in New York at the start of the United States lecture tour that brought him to San Francisco in 1882. Many flocked to Platt's Hall to hear the famed intellectual dandy, but he was faulted for his nasal voice and monotonous speaking style. Wilde still managed to have a great time on his visit west, dining with socialites and drinking his hosts under the table during a party in his honor at the Bohemian Club.

only has [Wilde] no thought, he is no thinker," Bierce hooted. "His lecture is mere verbal ditchwater—meaningless, trite, and without coherence."[11]

Wilde got back a little of his own by answering, when someone asked his impression of San Francisco's scenery: "Italy without its art."[12] Still, he apparently had a splendid several weeks in San Francisco, despite the nasty reviews. (He also had a few good ones.) His talks were well-attended, and offstage he enjoyed a visit to Chinatown, a long night of feasting and drinking with local writers at the Bohemian Club, and the gilded hospitality of the city's rich and faddish—who hung on his every *bon mot*. He also created a mini-vogue for his favorite blossom: the sunflower.

Like many international luminaries, Wilde made only one visit to California. A foreign celebrity who enchanted San Francisco and returned to it again and again was Sarah Bernhardt, the legendary French actress. The "Divine Sarah" ventured west for the first time in 1887 on her second tour of the United States. By then her genius was a matter of international record as were her rail-thin figure, scandalous ancestry (she was the daughter of a prostitute), son born out of wedlock, and fiery, independent temperament.

When Bernhardt's private rail car pulled into Oakland on May 15, 1887, a crowd of reporters awaited her. In the throng was an instantly-smitten *Chronicle* correspondent who described the forty-two-year-old Sarah as a "slender, graceful woman" with "light-brown hair (or was it red?) . . . artistically disarranged over and about a low, broad forehead (or was it high?) . . . [and] a pair of large, long, blue-gray eyes (or were they violet—or green?)." Bernhardt confided her opening night jitters to this scribe. "I have . . . been informed," she declared, "of all American audiences that of San Francisco is the most critical and exacting."[13]

Sarah had nothing to fear. Today her acting style would probably seem florid or hammy. But in her prime she was acclaimed as thoroughly modern—passionate and magnetic, but devoid of chest-thumping bombast. When she opened in Sardou's *Fedora* at the Baldwin, the reviewers were at her feet. The *Chronicle* dubbed Bernhardt "a phenomenon, one of those rare productions of nature that flash across an era and show us what can really be created." The *Call* found her "matchless," a woman whose "genius follows art to the ultimate." And yet another critic marveled over how "art so famed . . . should be so simple, so easy, so natural."[14]

Over the next two weeks, Bernhardt and company ran through (in

Three stars with San Francisco box office appeal: the "emotional actress" Clara Morris, famed for her realistic stage suffering (opposite top); *the vivacious Irish-born Ada Rehan* (opposite bottom), *whose milky beauty was likened to that of women in Gainsborough's portraits; and the one and only "Quand Même," Sarah Bernhardt* (left), *pictured here dressed for battle in Victor Hugo's Hernani.*

French) a sampler of her greatest hits (*La Dame aux Camélias, Adrienne Lecouvreur, Theodora*) and took in the magnificent sum of $41,000 at the box office. The actress charmed San Francisco on her off hours too, as she explored the city with journalists at her heels. She made a point of attending a theater in Chinatown and reacted to Chinese opera with a rare measure of cross-cultural respect and artistic empathy. She also raised eyebrows by visiting opium dens.

Having added San Francisco to her list of conquests, Bernhardt returned in April 1891 to play *Jeanne d'Arc, La Tosca,* and *Cleopatra* opposite one of France's great leading men, Constant Coquelin. Again the praise was lavish, and again Bernhardt's offstage exploits included a stop in Chinatown. This time, she delighted her Chinese colleagues by launching into a one-woman impersonation of their art form. "Her extraordinary powers of mimicry were never more thoroughly tested than here," wrote an *Examiner* reporter. "She had the wailing, jumbled music of the Chinese orchestra, with its wheezy, halting passages, down to life, and then she began the Chinese dance. It simply sent the house into convulsions."[15]

Bernhardt was one of the few top stars who refused to do the bidding of the Theatrical Syndicate, resulting in her being barred from some of the nation's largest halls. But she kept on touring America—sometimes performing in a tent, if necessary. Her warmth toward San Francisco remained constant. She made an emotional journey back in May 1906 just after the cataclysmic earthquake and on a 1913 tour made an appearance before two thousand inmates at nearby San Quentin Prison. She last played San Francisco in July 1918, by then a frail but majestic guest star with a vaudeville company. Upon Bernhardt's death in 1923 at age seventy-nine, San Francisco writer Annie Laurie paid tribute: "What generosity, what prodigal lavishness, what kindness of heart, what gaiety of spirits. . . . [Bernhardt] gathered San Francisco—the whole of it, in the palms of those delicious pointed little hands of hers, and hugged it to her heart."[16]

San Francisco's ardor for opera stars could be even more lavish than its worship of great actors. Some singers inspired a fascination bordering on fanaticism—as in the case of Italian soprano Adelina Patti.

Talent, wealth, sex appeal: Adelina Patti had it all, and she flaunted it. The world-renowned prima donna premiered locally at the Grand Opera House in March 1884 with Colonel John Henry Mapleson's Opera Troupe. Hearing of her arrival at the luxurious Palace Hotel, crowds thronged the

A dazzling star of the Daly Company, Fanny Davenport, like Sarah Bernhardt, found success in the romantic comedies and historical dramas of French playwright Victorien Sardou. But Davenport played them in English while Bernhardt never strayed from French, her native tongue, even while on tour in the United States.

SARONY.   680 BROADWAY.

FANNY DAVENPORT.

Appearances by Adelina Patti triggered riots and, in one case, an anarchist's bomb attack. In quieter moments, the Italian soprano—who demanded $5,000 in cash before each of her performances—retired to her Northern California ranch to commune with nature.

lobby. When tickets for her engagement went on sale, a near-riot erupted.

In his memoirs, Colonel Mapleson told how Patti fans smashed in the Opera House's glass doors, tore apart its box office, and overturned potted plants. Opening night triggered another mob scene: the expensive ball gowns of society ladies got torn in the crush, and some ticketholders could not get through the jostling crowd to take their seats.[17]

Newspapers clucked over Patti-madness: "How many went to hear her voice?" demanded an *Argonaut* correspondent. "She has become a spectacle like Jumbo or any other freak." Patti's vocal prowess took a back-seat to her jewels: "I doubt if twenty women in the house heard the music in the ballroom scene. *La diva* treated the house to a view of as many of her diamonds as she could carry without being brought in on trestles."[18]

Patti remained a darling of the smart set, returning to San Francisco periodically for thirty years—and for more than one "farewell" appearance. Local response remained frenzied—never more so than in 1887, when she sang *Lucia di Lammermoor* at the Grand Opera House. As the opera ended, J. A. Hodges, a seventy-year-old socialist agitator, lobbed a bomb onstage. If it had gone off, half of San Francisco society (and a gallery full of commonfolk) could have been wiped out. But the device sputtered and died, and Patti tripped out for an encore—blissfully unaware of how close she'd come to playing her final death scene.

Other opera favorites who captured San Francisco during this era included Nellie Melba, Luisa Tetrazzini, Eugenia Mantelli (whose accompanist, Gaetano Merola, would later play an important role in the city's operatic history), and Enrico Caruso. Meanwhile, local music-lovers remained attuned to those California singers who blossomed into international divas.

Perhaps the best known native opera star was Sibyl Sanderson, the beautiful daughter of a California Supreme Court judge. Sanderson grew up in San Francisco high society, sang at private events, and went to Paris to study voice while still a teenager. In France, her crystalline soprano beguiled composer Jules Massenet. Taking her on as a pupil, Massenet wrote several great operas for her—including his masterpiece, *Manon*.

With Maestro Massenet's help, Sanderson's career took off like a rocket in Europe. But by the time she ventured back to the U.S., her prime had passed. *Call* critic Blanche Partington offered a typically cool assessment of Sanderson's San Francisco debut: "From her work in 'Manon'

Nellie Melba, the famed Australian soprano, sang at opera houses all over the world and was heralded long in advance of her first appearance in San Francisco. She is pictured here as Marguerite in Gounod's Faust.

52

last night, Mme Sanderson cannot sing now, whatever she may have done once. The voice has gone, the control has gone, and only once . . . did her song give any evidence of the kind of thing that drew Paris and St. Petersburg to her feet a few years ago. . . . Though she is 'of ours,' it must be regretfully owned that Sybil Sanderson has no place in grand opera."[19]

Emma Nevada, a native of the Gold Rush town of Nevada City, California, fared better. She too studied in Europe, finding early success in the opera houses of Paris and Italy. But Nevada had the good fortune to come back to San Francisco in 1884 while still in her twenties, and she won high praise as a soprano with Colonel Mapleson's star-studded troupe. The next year "the California Songbird" was back again to inaugurate the new Alcazar Theater. As the *Chronicle* described it, "In spite of the wretched weather a long line of ladies and gentlemen stood for over four hours in the rain awaiting with what patience they might, a turn to secure tickets. . . . The indications are that the opening of this magnificent theater will be a success and that the reception accorded to Mme Nevada-Palmer will be a triumphant ovation." The paper was right on both counts.[20]

With all the divas, matinee idols, touring opera companies, and road shows passing through, was there any room in San Francisco for resident opera and theater ensembles? Yes, though less and less. Since the national entertainment scene was glutted with touring attractions of all types, what local mortals could compete with the high-wattage glow of international celebrities? The Industrial Age was gaining momentum, and with it came the "bigger is better" mentality that would pervade all aspects of public life in America in the century to come.

As it expanded in population and economic influence, San Francisco felt compelled to prove it was no frontier outpost, that it was just as *au courant* as East Coast and European culture capitols twice its size. It became essential to introduce the latest meteoric sensations from those cities—whether they arrived stale or spectacular—and many of these artists, in turn, regarded San Francisco as an imperative tour stop.

But in the face of daunting odds, some determined producers did try to form resident theater and opera companies that would belong exclusively to San Francisco. In the dramatic arena, only the Alcazar Theater's stock company (which we shall consider later) would last long. As for opera, there was one shining example of a homegrown outfit with staying power: the beloved Tivoli.

Native Californian Sibyl Sanderson, pictured here as the title character in Thais, *enjoyed a successful career in Europe but her voice was past its peak when she returned to San Francisco.* Thais *was one of several operas composed for her by her mentor, Jules Massenet.*

The Tivoli:
A Home for Light Opera

In May 1878 a comic opera by the new team of playwright W. S. Gilbert and composer Arthur Sullivan premiered in London. A witty satire of the British Navy graced with many hummable melodies, *HMS Pinafore* was soon all the rage. Word of its triumph reached American producers quickly: finally a lighthearted opera in English that any neophyte could understand and enjoy! Within months, two bootleg versions of *Pinafore* debuted in the States: one in Boston, the other in opera-loving, trend-setting San Francisco. The buoyant show proved to be a theatrical wonder. Like the earlier musical fairy extravaganza *The Black Crook* and the daring action drama *Mazeppa*, it seized the civic imagination ferociously. Numerous San Francisco theaters ran competing productions of it, and according to present-day *Chronicle* critic Robert Commanday's calculations, at least a third of the city's more than 230,000 residents rushed to see it.[1] A romp with dashing military officers and comely young damsels, it was just the ticket to lift spirits at the end of an economically troubled decade.

But *Pinafore* meant more to San Francisco than just another hit show. As the first major attraction of the Tivoli Opera House, it successfully inaugurated an important new home for modestly-priced, locally-produced operetta and opera. Other musical stages of the era were certainly larger, grander, and more elegant than the Tivoli, and brought in more diva superstars too. But none would thrive as long, or offer as many performances, or inspire as much affection and loyalty as this spirited, family-run establishment.

The Tivoli's *Pinafore* was a case of the right property at the right theater at exactly the right time. But San Francisco saw several other *Pinafore*s first: the initial one by the Alice Oates New English Opera Company at the Bush Street Theater (formerly the Alhambra), another at the Standard Theater starring local favorite Emelie Melville, yet another at the Grand Opera House, plus two "juvenile" runs—one with a padded cast of some two hundred youngsters. Tony Pastor's troupe trucked in the satirical *Canal Boat Pinafore*. Even anti-Chinese agitator Denis Kearny and his Workingman's Party got into the act with their own *Pinafore*

"The Tivoli was the most democratic house of amusement in the world. It has never had any stars, all of its plays being produced by its own stock company, no outside organization ever having taken possession of the stage. Although special talent was sometimes featured, equal consideration was invariably accorded to every member of the company. There are few persons and few families in San Francisco who have not at sometime been counted among the Tivoli's audiences. The millionaire came in and dropped into a seat beside the laboring man, and did not count his dignity grown less by so doing— a common love of music drawing them both."

"History of the Tivoli Opera House, 1879–99"
San Francisco Chronicle
August 27, 1899

TIVOLI OPERA HOUSE, 1879

burlesque at the Market Street Theater. (Kearny played the Admiral.)

It was up to Joseph Kreling, however, to put on a *Pinafore* everyone in town wanted to see. Kreling, born into a German family of upholsterers, had migrated from New York to San Francisco in 1875 at age twenty. Soon after his arrival he opened the Tivoli Gardens on the grounds of the Bowie home at Sutter and Stockton streets. At the beginning it was one of several *gemütlich* local resorts, an outdoor establishment where the good German beer and light classical music by the Vienna Ladies' Orchestra and the Spanish Students (a Mexican banjo-mandolin ensemble) were the chief attractions.

But Kreling had greater designs. He thought opera could exert mass appeal if offered in an unpretentious setting. In 1879 he and his brother John leased another lot on Eddy Street near Market and built a thousand-seat cabaret-style hall with a small gallery. The three-story white Victorian structure looked like an inviting private dwelling. The ticket prices were inviting too: twenty-five to fifty cents, a ten-cent refreshment coupon included.

Joe Kreling's *Pinafore* featured an onstage ship and the best performers from the other local productions. When it opened at the new Tivoli Opera House on July 3, 1879, the response was electric. Playing to full houses for 84 consecutive nights, the show became the city's longest-running stage attraction up to that point. The public kept calling it back, and by the end of the century *Pinafore* had logged 178 performances at the Tivoli. (The theater even spoofed itself with *The Wreck of the Pinafore,* a parody by local composer "Mrs. Church," which held forth briefly in the winter of 1879.)[2]

To prove that the Tivoli was more than a one-show wonder, Kreling quickly instituted a continuous schedule of production. His auditorium was soon *the* place in town to catch the latest in the increasingly popular genre of light opera: principally, shows in a blithe comic-romantic vein concocted by English, French, and German composers.

Many devoted patrons attended the Tivoli weekly, eager to catch the premiere of the American production of *The Mikado* (as big a smash as *Pinafore,* it was seen 179 times at the "Tiv") and all the subsequent Gilbert and Sullivan shows: *Patience, Pirates of Penzance, Trial by Jury,* among others. The works of French composer Jacques Offenbach also cast wide appeal (*The Brigands, La Belle Hélène*), as did those of Johann Strauss,

Emelie Melville (third from right) *starred in an early San Francisco production of* HMS Pinafore *at the Standard Theater. The Gilbert and Sullivan blockbuster, a beguiling spoof of English naval life, was given several bootleg productions soon after its London debut. In 1879 it became the first major presentation of the Tivoli Opera House, a new home for modestly priced, locally produced operetta and opera.*

Alexandre Lecocq, and Franz Von Suppe. Nor did the Tivoli turn its back on operas by local composers. W. W. Furst's warmly praised musicalization of *She*, the H. Rider Haggard novel, ran for 79 evenings.[3]

Because of the prevailing trend for "lightness" in all genres of entertainment, the Tivoli specialized in operetta rather than grand Italian opera. (Its major competition in this realm was the Winter Garden, a 2,500-seat hall that lasted from 1872 to 1883 but was always judged second best.) As historian John P. Young observed, "It was no longer possible to present *Norma* four or five nights in succession, and the music lovers had a surfeit, for the time being, of *Il Trovatore* and other operas which they knew by heart. . . . Although grand opera held its own . . . and never degenerated into a mere society function, the lighter forms of music were unquestionably gaining a stronghold on the popular taste."[4]

But the Tivoli did not entirely neglect more vocally demanding works.

In 1880 the establishment ventured into grand opera by presenting Gounod's *Faust* for 42 consecutive nights. Its success led to a hit production of Verdi's *Otello* soon after. At that point the hall was pulling in such crowds that Kreling enlarged it. The stage was expanded, viewing boxes added, racks for glasses installed on seatbacks, and tables removed to increase the seating capacity to roughly sixteen hundred.

Though more spacious and better-equipped than before, the Tivoli still eschewed ostentation and retained its democratic aura. The family feeling persisted, with all the Krelings pitching in to keep things running smoothly. Joe Kreling presided over the artistic business, translating most of the foreign language librettos into English himself. His wife and father helped out too, and his brothers William, John, and Martin tended the bars and the box office.

The Tivoli became a social epicenter, a congenial home away from home where San Franciscans from many walks of life could hear pleasing music, order a sandwich or a plate of fresh oysters or pastries from a friendly waiter in a white-starched apron, sip on a beer, and hobnob. Minstrel favorites Billy Emerson and Charlie Reed, pugilists Jim Corbett and John L. Sullivan, wealthy families like the Floods and the Baldwins rubbed elbows in the bar with "ordinary" citizens. Democracy extended to

The interior of the Tivoli Opera House, built in 1879, provided an attractive, congenial setting for San Francisco's elite and "ordinary" citizens to hobnob. Politicians rubbed elbows with prizefighters, and society grande dames munched sandwiches alongside seamstresses. Many of the Tivoli's loyal fans returned week after week to catch the wide array of musical attractions offered there.

The musical She ran for seventy-nine performances at the Tivoli. It was adapted by San Francisco composer W. W. Furst from the 1887 H. Rider Haggard novel, a mystery-romance set in Africa that, according to the psychologist C. G. Jung, exemplified the "anima" concept.

the stage as well: the Tivoli never adopted a star system and cast all shows from its sizable resident stock company. There was also room for out-of-town singers who found themselves at loose ends after a tour—if their singing was up to the Tivoli's standards.

And just what were its standards? From 1880 to 1900 the Tivoli produced consecutive runs of over one hundred music-theater works, ranging from *Cinderella* to *Aida*—and stayed dark for only 40 nights total. (In contrast, the Grand Opera House presented only 255 nights of opera in the same timespan.)[5] Given the incredible volume of production activity and the reliance on local talent, could the musical quality have remained high?

In his memoir, *In Our Second Century*, Jerome Hart suggests that

performances at the Tivoli "were never as good as old San Franciscans like to believe; but it had a fine orchestra, and a chorus which was rather mechanical but quite dependable."[6] But other ear-witness accounts give the Tivoli company more credit. It boasted some outstanding singers, including the star tenor Harry Gates and the beloved soprano Gracie Plaisted. And many gifted beginners and entire opera clans came up via the Tivoli ranks, including the Stockmeyers (a singing father and his six daughters), the young soprano Alice Nielsen, and the much-admired Valerga clan: prima donna Ida, tenor Richard, soubrette Tillie, and supporting player Kitty.

Such top-notch guest stars as Emelie Melville and conductor-composer Pietro Mascagni also appeared. And among the busy musical directors at the Tivoli was Gustav Hinrichs, who was later praised as doing more for San Francisco than any other musician. In addition to conducting operas, he led symphony orchestras, chamber music quartets, and choral groups.[7]

An era ended in 1887 when the overworked Joe Kreling died, still in his thirties. But the Tivoli continued to prosper under the ownership of Joe's widow, Ernestine, and her capable general manager, William "Doc" Leahy—who also became her second husband. Together they inaugurated an annual grand opera season. Though the nine-to-twelve-week series of Italian and German works raised production expenses considerably, the Tivoli maintained the same low ticket prices it had always charged.

Leahy built a new Tivoli in 1903 after the city condemned the old structure as a firetrap. Situated across from the popular Old Poodle Dog Restaurant on the corner of Eddy and Mason streets, the relocated Tivoli was a bit fancier and more formal than the one it replaced—to the chagrin of some old-timers. (Interestingly, Hollywood based the sets for the 1936 film *San Francisco* on the second Tivoli Opera House rather than the original one.)

In 1905 Leahy's Tivoli scored one of the city's greatest musical *coups* by presenting the United States debut of the Italian coloratura soprano Luisa Tetrazzini. La Tetrazzini had been stranded in Mexico while on tour and eagerly accepted Leahy's offer of train fare and a singing engagement. Opera fans went mad for the diva's voice, which in the words of one local critic could "scale such airy ladders of sound, sending from each silver rung a spray of liquid pearls."[8] The Tivoli stand helped catapult Tetrazzini to success at New York's Metropolitan Opera.

Not long after this triumph, the 1906 earthquake and fire devastated the Tivoli (along with most other local theaters). It took seven years for Leahy to rebuild the facility, which he inaugurated on March 12, 1913, with a thrilling all-star concert by Tetrazzini, Mary Garden, and the Chicago Opera Company. (The glossy program book for the event boasted that the Tivoli "was the only theater of the past or present with 12,142 consecutive performances to its credit.")

This milestone moved some longtime patrons to reminisce about the old Tivoli. "From roof to floor [it] was a storehouse of memories to last night's throng," wrote an *Examiner* reporter. "Generations after generations of San Franciscans can trace some of their happiest nights and recollections to its doors. . . . The like of it never was before in San Francisco, and with that, rather stunned by it all, one must let it go."[9]

The writer's remarks were prophetic. A year later no Tivoli Opera House existed in San Francisco—old or new. Leahy decided to turn his just-built auditorium into a moving picture theater. Why? He blamed the new diversion of movies for diminishing the Tivoli attendance and drying up his profit. And he denounced the city's plan to construct a municipally subsidized opera house instead of aiding his already existing one.[10]

Announcement of the Tivoli conversion elicited an outpouring of tributes from San Franciscans who had grown up there. Local poet Mabel Porter Pitts expressed her regrets in a long, sentimental ode that praised "Your old back-breaking, hard seated chairs / Your quaint, little, dark nestling boxes upstairs / Where many a man, under stress of the play / Has said foolish things he regretted next day."[11]

Others mourned the loss of a certain musical ambience the city would never reclaim. The Tivoli's ability to consistently offer crowd-pleasing versions of both grand and comic opera—at low prices, in a relaxed and unformidable setting, with fine local singers and musicians—was probably unequaled in the country. Perhaps it was only possible in the culturally populist environment of pre-1906 San Francisco.

In its prime the Tivoli had been looked upon as an extension of the family parlor, never as a highbrow arts palace. "You almost always knew who was going to sit next to you at the old Tivoli," recalled newspaperman George M. Poultney. "In fact, you knew most everyone in the house."[12] Thomas Nunan, another journalist, spoke for many of his generation when he wrote, "The old Tivoli was something more than a mere amusement place. It was the musical life and inspiration of the community."[13]

Guest stars at the Tivoli included conductor-composer Pietro Mascagni (opposite top), *coloratura Luisa Tetrazzini* (middle), *and Gustav Hinrichs* (bottom), *a popular Tivoli music director who conducted orchestras and choral groups throughout San Francisco. Ida Valerga* (below) *was one of four Valerga siblings to rise through the Tivoli ranks. She is pictured here in* Il Trovatore *in 1887.*

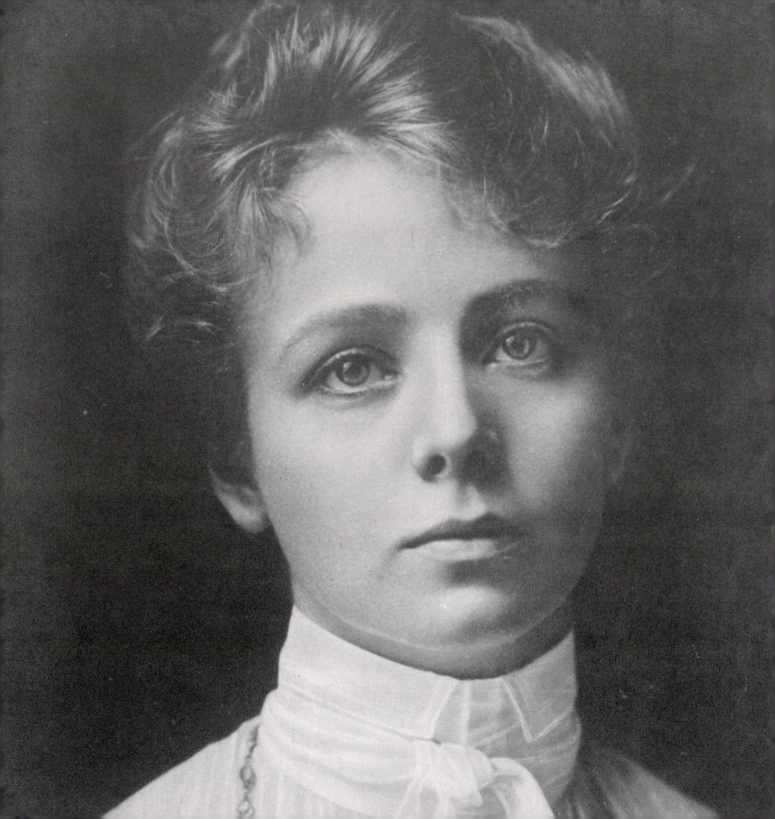

Hiss the Villain, Cheer the Girl:
The Age of Melodrama

The plots usually depicted tragic misfortunes, resistance to brutal adversaries, and ultimately the triumph of love and goodness over evil and degradation. The protagonist, often a comely young woman with dewy eyes and long flowing hair, tended to be virtuous and poor, the villain mustachioed and rich. Swept up in the emotions swirling over the footlights, viewers joined in the action—vocally and viscerally. A prototypical melodrama, according to theater historian Robert Toll, offered theatergoers the perfect "outlet for their feelings and emotions—a chance to scream, to laugh, to gasp, and to cry."[1]

Odds were that anyone attending a "serious" play in San Francisco in the last decades of the nineteenth century saw some kind of melodrama: that is, a play of broad action and characterization, with clearly-defined heroes and villains, unlikely twists of fate, and a happy-ever-after ending for the righteous and pure.

Melodramas had prospered, of course, back in the Gold Rush era, and they later became the paradigmatic form for much of what Hollywood produced. But from the 1880s to the early 1900s, before literary innovators like Eugene O'Neill arrived on the scene, the melodrama (in all its myriad forms) dominated American playwrighting almost entirely.

Not that the melodrama form was monochromatic. There were the David Belasco–style "sensation" melodramas with realistic effects evoking fire and snowstorm, avalanche and shipwreck, and exotic locales—as in Belasco's own atmospheric *Stranglers of Paris*, seen at the Grand Opera House in 1885. And there were the scores of "frontier" melodramas, such as the sentimental *In Old Kentucky* and, in a California vein, Clay M. Greene's oft-revived *M'Liss, or The Child of the Sierras*, based on a Bret Harte sketch about a spunky mountain girl determined to get an education.

More enduringly popular were the romantic melodramas (which man to marry?) and the ubiquitous domestic melodramas, exemplified by the perennial hit *East Lynne* and Steele Mackaye's *Hazel Kirke*—a favorite with ladies who sympathized with Hazel's troubles. (*Hazel* really heaped on the travails: disowned daughter, penniless husband, blind father, repossessed

"[Society] wants melodrama, and wants it just as thunderous and just as lurid as it can be made. It wants Kentucky Girls performing the impossible in the nick of time. It wants buzz-saws, and mill wheels and spark-sputtering railroad trains, juggernauts of all sizes, shapes and varieties: low-rumbling villainies, spine-shivering situations, ecstatic virtue, soul-thrilling heroism, wildly-impassioned love-making. . . . [The] people want to have their spleens affected with a new sensation."

San Francisco Examiner
May 20, 1894

63

MAUDE ADAMS

mill, attempted suicide—capped off, of course, by a happy ending.) And one can't overlook the granddaddy of them all, *Uncle Tom's Cabin*, based on the abolitionist novel by Harriet Beecher Stowe. The most popular and durable of American melodramas, *Uncle Tom* did fine business in San Francisco (in many versions) for more than six decades.

As heightened, morally unambiguous depictions of "real life" with characters that common people could identify with, melodramas were scorned by many critics but powerfully attractive to the fast-growing mass of working-class theatergoers. Whether they celebrated the exploits of Davy Crockett or tested the virtue of a sewing girl, melodramas were essentially populist fantasies, a reassuring mix of vicarious thrills and moral bromides attuned to an era when the country was rushing pell-mell into a disorienting future of industrialism and urbanity. Charging "people's prices" that ranged from ten cents to a dollar, San Francisco's playhouses kept a steady supply of them before an insatiable public—the same public that was also devouring dime adventure stories and romantic novels.

The resident troupe quartered at the Alcazar Theater thrived on the more genteel manifestations of the melodrama form. Located at O'Farrell Street between Stockton and Powell, the Alcazar was erected by *Chronicle* publisher Michael DeYoung in 1885 as a lecture and concert hall. Architecturally it had some outstanding features: decor in an extravagant "Moorish" style; ornaments of gold, bronze, and silver; and seven hundred gas jets lit by that amazing new invention—electricity. Operatic soprano Emma Nevada opened the house with a sold-out vocal recital, but classical music was quickly overtaken by drama.

In 1886 George Wallenrod assumed management of the Alcazar and installed its initial stock acting company. Wallenrod was a sharp businessman who knew, as did other successful producers of the era, that variety and flexibility were the keys to economic survival in the modern entertainment marketplace. He kept business at the Alcazar brisk by changing the playbill often, plugging in engagements by touring companies, and renting the house out to other local troupes now and then.

But the Alcazar's main attraction was its fine stock ensemble, the only one in town with any longevity since the demise of the California and Baldwin companies. Standard fare at the Alcazar consisted of American melodramas and farces interspersed with worthy new English plays (by such contemporary wordsmiths as George Bernard Shaw, Arthur Wing

Pinero, Oscar Wilde, and James Barrie), along with the occasional older classic. The Alcazar players generated the kind of audience loyalty that the veteran singers at the Tivoli Opera House commanded. And, though never top-ranked artistically, the theater held its own in a cutthroat market.

The press was supportive but candid about the caliber of the shows. The *News Letter* pronounced the Alcazar "very successful in catering to the lenient tastes of what constitutes a very large proportion of theatergoers."[2] And the *Morning Call* concluded, "All the engagements here, good, bad, or indifferent, seem alike to please the people in attendance, for the auditorium is crowded to the doors every night."[3]

The Alcazar put up a new production every week or so, starring the season's current Leading Man and Leading Lady or, on occasion, hired-in "big name" actors like Nat C. Goodwin, Eddie Foy, and Milton Nobles. The well-honed company assumed the supporting and minor roles. Again, this system provided a great education for the novice actors on hand. One gifted Alcazar alumnus was Maude Adams, the lovely young ingenue who had started out with the Baldwin Company. (After Charles Frohman discovered Adams, she went on to become one of the nation's favorite leading ladies, beguiling Broadway as the first Peter Pan.) Other notable players included the young Nance O'Neil, Bertram Lytell, Joseph R. Grismer and his wife Phoebe Davies, and Lincoln Stockwell. (Stockwell would go on to head his own stock company for several years and later run the city's leading Syndicate playhouse, the Columbia Theater.)

At a "family theater" like the Alcazar, fairly literate melodramas-of-virtue ruled. A typical "domestic" example was the 1890 production of *Woman Against Woman* by Frank Harvey. According to the *Chronicle*, the convoluted plot centered on one Bessie Barton, a young working girl who performs a selfless act on her sister's behalf only to face nasty rumors, a soured marriage, the death of her child, and the unemployment of her increasingly "morose and brutal" husband. In the end, of course, "everything turns out satisfactorily, and Bessie's heroism is rewarded by peace and happiness at least." The script was "interlarded" with "many humorous situations and exciting episodes," and was deemed "the best domestic melodramatic effort of its clever author."[4]

Works by local playwrights also premiered at the Alcazar. One of the more intriguing was *The First Born*, a family melodrama by Francis Powers that was most likely the first professionally produced drama about Chinese

Americans. Avidly researched by Powers in Chinatown and set near Sacramento Street and Bartlett Alley, it was praised as an "accurate" portrait and "manifold panorama" of life among San Francisco's Chinese citizens—though the speaking parts were handled by Caucasians in slant-eyed makeup and the Chinese cast members stayed in the background as "local color." (Walter Belasco, brother of David, was cast as a Jewish peddler.) A six-week hit in San Francisco during the spring of 1897, *The First Born* was later optioned by David Belasco and eventually produced in New York. Powers went on to give his version of Mexican life in the play *Mother Earth,* another Alcazar premiere.

The Alcazar was one of the few local theaters to outlast the next crippling depression, which hit in the early 1890s. By then Wallenrod was long gone, but other sharp managers, including the crack team of Milton

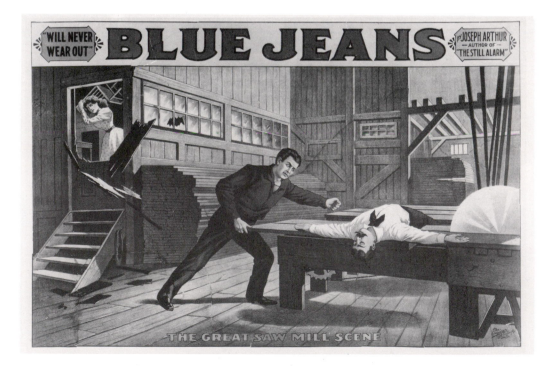

"WILL NEVER WEAR OUT" BLUE JEANS by JOSEPH ARTHUR — AUTHOR OF — "THE STILL ALARM"

THE GREAT SAW MILL SCENE

Mayer and Fred Belasco, kept the theater busy right up to the eve of the 1906 earthquake. The quake wrecked the theater, but didn't finish off the Alcazar. Its stock company continued on at the New Alcazar, erected in 1907 at Sutter and Steiner streets, and then relocated in 1911 to a third Alcazar at 260 O'Farrell Street. The latter playhouse presented drama intermittently until its demolition in 1961. In 1976 the Alcazar name was conferred on yet a fourth theater, at 650 Geary Street.

The Alcazar always stressed variety, but one important San Francisco producer went to extremes with sensation melodrama. He was Walter Morosco, a former circus acrobat who came to town in the early 1880s and established himself as a masterful producer of B-grade entertainment. In 1885 Morosco took over Union Hall, a venerable auditorium at Third and Howard streets, and served up unique double bills at bargain prices.

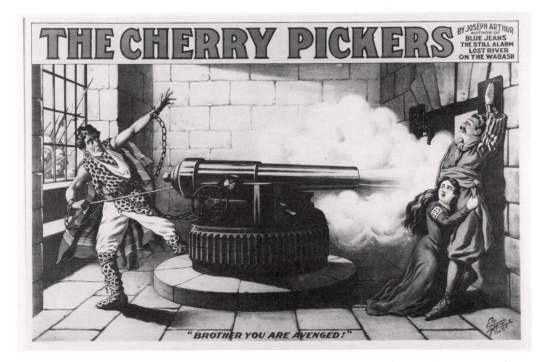

The Alcazar Theater (below), which opened in 1885, fostered the talents of many promising young actors. Its stock company ran longer than any in San Francisco theater history. Oakland native Nance O'Neil (opposite), born Gertrude Lamson in 1874, went on to a successful Broadway and screen career after a debut stint with the Alcazar company. Her father, a well-known East Bay auctioneer, considered her ambitions "sinful" and refused to speak to his daughter after she made her professional debut at the theater. Nance O'Neil was nineteen years old at the time.

Viewers got a lot at the Union for twenty cents: two hours of vaudeville acts followed by two more hours of full-throttle melodrama.

In 1894 the ambitious Morosco abandoned the Union and gained control of the Grand Opera House, much to the disdain of some local critics who looked down on him for hawking cheap thrills at such a respected facility. The city's largest theater had been managed unsuccessfully by numerous men and had seen everything from Shakespearean tragedies to full-tilt operas to gaudy musicals like *The Black Crook*. Morosco certainly had something else in mind. He assembled a stock company and for the next five years presented an array of "spectacular" dime melodramas that seized the public imagination with astonishingly realistic scenic effects.

When Morosco promised thrills, he delivered them unstintingly. During the suspense melodrama *The Danger Signal*, an express train rumbled across the Opera House stage at fifty miles an hour. *The Operator* went further with the wreck of both a train *and* a bona fide steamship. *The Pace that Kills* boasted a hair-raising stampede of ten thoroughbred horses.[5]

But Morosco's *pièce de résistance* had to be *A Flag of Truce*, an 1895 adventure saga set in a quarry. According to the *Call* notice, the climactic scene featured an explosion set by demolition experts and a hoisting derrick "of actual size and power lifting a full twenty feet from the stage a massive boulder of a ton's weight." Under this boulder lay the quivering hero "in deadly peril, while the villain [trifled] with the machinery, which [could] make it fall and crush him to powder." The show ended with a blast that obscured the stage "in dustclouds of powdered stone." Morosco's actors—among them Lucille La Verne and Theodore Roberts, both future silent film stars—were a plucky lot who deserved medals for bravery.[6]

Critics greeted Morosco's hardcore theatricality with skepticism, but soon acknowledged its effect on audiences. (It also affected Morosco. Reportedly, he could often be found in the back row of the theater weeping over the predicament of a beleaguered heroine.) These entertainments drew like gangbusters; at one point Morosco was arrested for seating patrons in the aisles. And it wasn't just the "man on the street" who loved lurid melodramas with titles like *The Red Spider, The Great Diamond Robbery*, and *The Ages of Sin*. They were hits with society folk too.

As an *Examiner* correspondent noted in 1898, "The fad is so growing that the real 'first night audience' is rapidly being transferred from the theaters, where a great deal of stupidity has been ladled out recently at high rates, to Morosco's Grand Opera House, where the performance is never stupid, no matter what else may be said of it."[7] The *Bulletin* congratulated Morosco for the "enterprise and sagacity" that had earned him a "colossal fortune."[8]

While pouring on the blood and thunder, Morosco occasionally produced hit comedies and turned to weepies like *Article 47,* a Creole love melodrama starring the well-known "emotional actress" Maude Granger. In 1899, after making a mint and presenting 5,635 consecutive melodrama performances, Morosco made a sudden bid for greater respectability by dissolving his stock company, upping his ticket prices, and bringing grand opera back to the Grand Opera House—briefly but gloriously.[9] He then offered a season of light opera and extravaganzas (at only fifteen to seventy cents per ticket) and hosted one of Sarah Bernhardt's local engagements. In July 1901 Morosco retired and left for New York, where he died unexpectedly several months later. (His adopted son and protégé, Oliver Morosco, would become a successful producer in Los Angeles and on Broadway.)

Though Morosco had eased the Grand Opera out of the melodrama business, the form persisted. In the early years of the century, melodramas were the mainstay both of the new Central Theater and of a stock company led by Bertha Creighton and Herschel Mayall at the old Alhambra, while they still popped up with regularity at the Alcazar.

Despite the obvious literary limitations of melodrama—the predictability, the absence of irony and moral complexity—its conventions have proved resilient. In his book *Stage to Screen,* A. Nicholas Vardac explores the profound impact this "realistic and romantic" style of theater would have on early Hollywood films. The first movies, in fact, were faithful adaptations of the live melodramas that audiences saw in San Francisco and other cities.[10] Even today, what are most television soap operas and miniseries if not topical domestic melodramas? And what are the latest action-adventure films but sensation melodramas with car, plane, and spaceship crashes instead of train wrecks?

Back in pre-earthquake San Francisco, theatergoers reveled in live melodrama at its most emotively and technically extravagant. But many drama critics were waiting impatiently for a new, more realistic, and revelatory kind of American stage literature to emerge.

Slummers' Paradise:
Joints, Dives & Variety Halls

During the Gold Rush years, San Francisco handily established its reputation as one of the most wide-open, morally lax, thrill-seeking cities in the Western Hemisphere—a burg where red-blooded men had continual access to gambling, liquor, prostitutes of various races, opium dens, street fights, and the kind of risqué girlie shows that decent, God-fearing folk steered clear of. But as the city doubled in size, its seamier aspects were counterbalanced somewhat by the expanding number of religious institutions and families. Newspapers, religious leaders, and reform-minded politicians began pressing for laws that would curb illicit and objectionable amusements.

Such campaigns to "clean up" San Francisco occurred periodically. In 1869 the *Call* urged passage of a law that banned the employment of women in melodeons, dance halls, and concert saloons. It was enacted but completely ignored. A similar ordinance, passed in 1876 at the urging of the *Chronicle*, met with a similar fate. In 1892 the City Council finally tried a tactic that had some short-lived success: it voted to end the sale of liquor in theatrical establishments.

Yet, right up to and well after the 1906 earthquake, San Francisco offered plenty of raw iniquity to anyone looking for it. And one did not have to look far. Two primary nightlife areas—the notorious Barbary Coast district around Kearny Street and several raucous blocks of Market Street known as "The Line"—offered a generous selection of gambling parlors, whorehouses, and "deadfalls" (the raunchiest bars). For a dime or the price of a drink, a fellow could wander into variety theaters, dance halls, basement saloons, even canvas tents lit with flaming torches and catch some very diverting acts.

As in Gold Rush times, most of these loud, smoky dives appealed to men—and the "shady" ladies who worked in them. But now there were many more such places than before, and their stage bills changed often with the whims of show business. Though new crazes often bubbled up in these unsavory venues, journalists tended not to report them—except those bohemian scribes who savored the colorful atmosphere and cheap booze,

"The Barbary Coast is the haunt of the low and vile of every kind. The petty thief, the house burglar, the tramp, the whore monger, lewd women, cut-throats and murderers, all are found there. Dance houses and concert saloons, where blear-eyed men and faded women drink vile liquor, smoke offensive tobacco, engage in vulgar conduct, sing obscene songs, and say and do everything to heap upon themselves degradation, unrest and misery, are numerous."

B. E. Lloyd
Lights and Shades of San Francisco
1876

BELLES OF THE BELLA UNION

and the travel writers chronicling their general impressions of the city. What was a San Francisco travelogue, after all, without a descripton of "exotic" Chinatown or a portrait of the wild, wicked Barbary Coast?

After an 1875 stay in the city, *Scribner's Monthly* correspondent Samuel Williams described the Barbary Coast scene. Some saloons, he wrote, "have organs that invite patrons to dally. . . . [They] play overtures, marches and tasteful variations. Other bars have bands, still others pianos. And some, in addition to a band, keep a female staff capable of waking thirst in a stone." The underground clubs he described as "subterranean spaces . . . illuminated by skylights covered with heavy little circles of glass set into iron gratings. Spread across the sidewalks, and with artificial light below, these bits of glass give the effect of tiny wells of flame."

As for the dance halls, Williams found them "merely a pretext by which women are employed to stimulate the sale of liquor. The music is outrageous, the dances crowded, and the police have not infrequently to descend to restore order. Thus these justly-famed infernos are a link between lower-class restaurants and the minstrel shows."[1]

When local daily newspapers paid any notice, they struck a similar tone. A November 16, 1890, *Examiner* article defensively titled "Good or Bad? San Francisco's Morals: They Might Be Better, but They Might Be a Great Deal Worse" lumped together all saloon performers as "a vile lot, personally and artistically, with hard, degraded faces. Their 'whittle jokes,' accommodated to the desires of the audiences and their own sense of humor, are hardly of a sort to bear telling about."

Williams and the *Examiner* were both right. But there was more to the Barbary Coast scene than they suggested. Plenty of clip joints used flirtatious waitresses and performers as bait to lure in (and rip off) drunken sailors and lumberjacks on a spree. And, certainly, much of the stage humor heard was crude and vulgar by nineteenth-century standards.

But some of the saloons and variety theaters near the waterfront hired lively and diverse acts featuring talented artists. They showcased up-and-coming young singers and comedians like Eddie Foy and the winning team of Ned Harrigan and Tony Hart, gave breaks to African American performers barred by racism from "legit" houses, and created a niche for budding novelty performers (magicians, dog trainers, you name it). Even so prudish an observer as B. E. Lloyd, writing in 1876, had to admit that "a young actress [now] playing before the most refined audiences in the

The top-ranked comic duo of Edward "Ned" Harrigan and Tony Hart often appeared at the Bush State Theater, the Alcazar, and other San Francisco venues in the 1880s. Before meeting up with Hart in Chicago, Harrigan spent years working the variety halls of San Francisco's Barbary Coast. The playlets he wrote for himself and Hart were early examples of American ethnic humor, gently poking fun at Italian, Irish, Jewish, German, and black working class life. Harrigan also penned many popular tunes of the era, including such folksy odes as "The Babies on Our Block" and "Maggie Murphy's Home."

United States . . . spent her younger years before the most vulgar and debased audiences in San Francisco." That was Lotta Crabtree, who to Lloyd's amazement had "passed through the filth unstained."[2]

Back in the 1850s when little Lotta played the Barbary Coast, blackface minstrelsy was all the rage. But from the 1870s through the 1890s performers tried out other gambits, shticks, and routines that would eventually find their way onto San Francisco's more respectable stages. The corny old banjo-on-my-knee minstrel revues that had been so popular were dying out, except those with uptown stars like San Francisco's own Billy Emerson and (eventually) those that featured bona fide African American performers rather than white men in black paint.

The newest fashion in the cabarets was a hodgepodge of uninhibited social dancing and high-kicking chorus numbers, knockabout slapstick and "blue" comedians, plus all manner of magic, juggling, animal acts, female and Chinese impersonators, quickie sensation dramas, and miniburlesques—including ribald parodies of legitimate shows like *HMS Pinafore* and *The Black Crook*, and stars like Sarah Bernhardt (often spoofed as "Sarah Heartburn"). Put it all together on one long bill and it was variety—the racy farm team for what would soon become major league vaudeville.

Every "minor" San Francisco showplace had its own flavor, from the utterly depraved to the near-genteel. Wandering down Battle Row, a particularly tough section of Kearny Street, a thrill-seeking visitor could sample more than one ambience. Near the waterfront was the bawdy Strassburg Music Hall, managed by a tall, dark beauty called Spanish Kitty. A couple of blocks south stood the Eureka Music Hall, a barn-like arena said to have some of the prettiest waitresses and best comedians in town, plus such suggestive dance acts as the Four Fleet Sisters (they all married members of the Navy) and little Jose Dupree. Within another few blocks, the busy Adelphi Saloon (probably the first to present a troupe of African American minstrels) and the rowdy Comique held forth.

But the dean of the Barbary Coast clubs was the venerable Bella Union, an amusement palace at Washington and Kearny streets that dated all the way back to 1849. Time did not stand still at the Bella Union. In 1880 the place was *au courant* in offering a wide array of acts. The playbill for August 16 promised: "The midgets, smallest men in the world; Baron Little Finger and Count Rosebud; Miss Lottie Elliott, champion skipping-rope dancer; Cummings and Harrington, monarchs of song and dance;

Lydia Thompson, an English burlesque performer, rounded up a troupe of hearty fair-haired dancers and toured them profitably across the United States—first in 1868, and numerous times thereafter. Thompson starred in the usual spoofs of operas and fairy stories, but she had a spectacular gimmick: she costumed herself and her chorus of "British Blondes" in leg-revealing white tights, attracting much publicity from scribes and much scorn from those who found a glimpse of stocking quite shocking indeed. In San Francisco, unsurprisingly, she was a big hit—and returned frequently into the 1890s with new regiments of blondes in tow.

73

Miss Zitella, the lightning change artist; John Gilbert, burlesque and character artist; Plus, a Production of the three-act sensational drama, 'LOST IN LONDON'."

The Bella Union entered a rocky period in 1880, when founder Samuel Tetlow shot his business partner in self-defense and left the business. But the club bounded back in 1887, after Ned Foster took control. The flamboyant Foster was an act on his own: He got around in a gaudy cart driven by a team of black Shetland ponies, and he kept a tall black bodyguard nicknamed Deacon Jones always at his side. He also took pride in his "stable" of pretty chorus girls. His "dodgers" (handbills) assured patrons that only women with "Lovely Tresses! Lovely Lips! Buxom Forms!" would be on display.[3]

The Bella Union's fiercest rival for a time was the Midway Plaisance (originally Jack Cremorne's), a joint on Market between Third and Fourth streets that saw many a knock-down, drag-out brawl—along with some exciting new dance fads. In the 1890s the Midway introduced the hip-jiggling hootchy-cootchy to San Francisco, performed by such experts as the Girl in Blue and the bellydancer Little Egypt, fresh from her triumph at the Chicago's World Fair.

Singers and dancers were ubiquitous in nightspots, but eccentric acts of all kinds thrived too. Among the more legendary Barbary Coast performers were the 280-pound comedienne Big Bertha and the Jack Sprat-like Oofty Goofty. Oofty Goofty appeared first as a Wild Man of Borneo in a freak show and then found success as a human punching bag; for fifty cents he'd let any comer smash him with a baseball bat. Bertha went on exhibit at the Midway Plaisance as Queen of the Confidence Women, publicly smoking a cigarette (a shocking act in itself) and giving bawdy accounts of her alleged adventures in crime.

This bizarre pair had their greatest triumph together in a burlesque of the balcony scene from *Romeo and Juliet*. The act relied heavily on physical abuse, and Bertha stopped doing it after a week—despite packed houses howling for more—because Oofty Goofty was too rough. Her solo follow-up was a parody of Adah Isaacs Menken's equestrienne performance in *Mazeppa*, which Bertha performed on a donkey instead of the customary horse. That act ended the night Bertha and her mount tumbled into the orchestra pit, nearly crushing several musicians.[4]

Such antics probably amused many San Franciscans and could be

*William F. Cody, the legendary fron-
tiersman known as "Buffalo Bill,"
brought his Wild West show to the Bay
Area several times in the early 1900s.
A frontier scout during the Civil War,
he acted in western melodramas,
including Ned Buntline's 1873 play
The Scouts of the Plains. In 1883 he
conceived a show of his own, which
became the prototype for a crowd-
pleasing genre of live Wild West entertainments. In this photo, he poses in
front of the old Oakland Tribune
building, around 1913, as members of
the show's cast look on.*

grudgingly tolerated by the others. But what got people up in arms was the rampant and blatant prostitution in the Barbary Coast (which sometimes involved the torture and enslavement of young women) and the girlie shows—or, as the *Examiner* described them, the "exhibitions of vulgarity, pruriency and immodesty."[5]

As a result of the influx and success of elaborate musical epics (*The Black Crook, Sinbad the Sailor, Aladdin's Lamp*) and of not-quite-wholesome all-gal troupes (Lydia Thompson and her British Blondes), the mere thought of women exposing their legs in flesh-colored tights no longer sent proper folk into a frenzy. Yet there was still the occasional storm over a naughty (for the time) act like Mabel Santley's English Burlesque Troupe. In 1879 Santley's blonde squad (and their manager, Michael Leavitt) got hauled into court. Their crime? Delivering an overly enthusiastic version of the French cancan, with too much leg showing. The *News Letter* of February 22 wrote Mabel and her crew off as "plain and mostly middle-aged. . . . The performance is unsufferably stupid, but tights are worn and limbs are shown, and bald heads and downy tikes will pay for this sort of thing." After a first-hand look at their act, a jury convicted Santley of indecent exposure and fined her $200.[6]

Displays like Santley's could get the local morals monitors very agitated. But by the 1880s the general perception of variety halls as sinkholes of sin began to slowly shift. A watershed of sorts was the *Chronicle's* 1881 decision to carry advertisements for the Bella Union and the Adelphi, a smart business move and an acknowledgment that some cabarets really did emphasize shows rather than vice. And by 1889 a *Chronicle* pundit could admit that "the dives are not all as black as some would paint them. "[7]

Actually, by that point quite a few variety halls existed that were not "dives" at all. The 1,200-seat Bijou, the Wigwam (where patrons heard opera arias between comedy routines), the Union (under Walter Morosco's management), the Market Street Theater, the Standard, Fern Hall, and the Fountain all offered variety fare but maintained decorum. (Maybe they displayed less flesh, or perhaps their surroundings made audiences more comfortable with it.) The Market Street even offered Saturday family matinees, charging a somewhat pricey admission of twenty-five cents for adults, fifteen cents for children.

Though San Francisco had a much more prolific nightlife than most

American cities its size, the widening popularity of variety reflected a national trend. As the American economy shifted from a rural-farming base to an urban-industrial base, working people were dropping some of their religious, cultural, and social inhibitions about theater and heading out more often for amusement. In San Francisco this led not only to the boom in melodrama, but also to the creation of a middle tier of variety and vaudeville establishments wedged comfortably between the conventional theaters and the low-down saloons.

It was a case of the more the merrier, because the wilder venues of the Barbary Coast and "The Line" kept right on going too. Men continued to crowd into town for shore leave and work breaks, titillated by San Francisco's global fame as the Port Said of the American West Coast. Drunken carousing reached a peak in 1890 when a record 3,117 establishments held municipal permits to sell liquor and roughly 2,000 more operated as "blind tigers" (speakeasies). That meant there was roughly one bar for every sixty San Francisco residents.[8]

As the booze flowed in the city's 500 or so turn-of-the-century dance and music saloons, the first strains of ragtime and jazz could be heard and the dances grew snappier, more athletic, and sexually suggestive. Even the devastating 1906 earthquake couldn't wipe out the Barbary Coast and its satellites.

Most of the bars and dance halls were fire traps, burning quickly in the postquake blaze. And in 1907, an outraged Catholic pastor named Terence Caraher launched a campaign to make sure a new Barbary Coast rife with prostitution, liquor, and hootchy-cootchy didn't rise from the ashes of the old one. But by 1910, some three hundred busy saloons and dance halls had already opened up within a six-block area around Pacific Street to make up for those destroyed in the conflagration.[9]

It took several more years and an all-out war on vice led by publisher William Randolph Hearst in his *San Francisco Examiner* to put an end to the Barbary Coast and its overspill. But until that happened, San Francisco lived up to its nickname of "Slummers' Paradise," a place with enough wine, women, and song for every taker. And despite those who would have it otherwise, Barbary Coast chronicler Herbert Asbury seems right in suggesting that many San Franciscans were secretly "proud of their city's reputation as the Paris of America and the wickedest town on the continent."[10]

The scandalously famous bellydancer Little Egypt performed in nightclubs up and down the Barbary Coast, where her tummy rolls and hip swivels caused a great stir. She is pictured here in 1893.

'Genuine Negroes':
African Americans Take the Stage

One day in 1893, a tall African American man in his late teens stopped at the corner of Market and O'Farrell streets to ask another black youth if he knew where to find a good "end man" for a minstrel act. The fellow doing the asking was Egbert Austin ("Bert") Williams; the stranger who answered him was George Walker.

This casual meeting between two journeyman entertainers led to a historic event: an alliance that would greatly boost the status of blacks in American show business. It is not insignificant that Williams and Walker, the first black stars of the Broadway musical stage, would find each other on the streets of San Francisco. Nor is it surprising that they spent the first years of their partnership performing in the city's multiracial saloons and variety halls, where people of various backgrounds could mingle freely.

Actually, African Americans had been contributing to San Francisco's dynamic cultural life, directly and indirectly, for decades. But it wasn't until the end of the last century that talented black artists like Williams and Walker could even dream of achieving the respect, status, and remuneration their white counterparts routinely enjoyed. Even in a milieu as racially diverse and relatively tolerant as San Francisco, blacks in all walks of life encountered bigotry on a daily basis. And the early entertainers among them faced a schizoid dilemma: To gain access to the stage they had to pretend to be African "exotics," anthropological specimens. Or they had to apply burnt cork makeup and copy white minstrels' distorted interpretations of "Southern Negro" behavior. The first blacks in show business were pressured to live *down* to the expectations created for them by other performers, to obliterate their own identities and masquerade as southern "plantation darkies" and northern "zip coons."

Beneath the skin, the African Americans who made their way to California were not so different from those of Latin American, Asian, and European heritage thronging the Gold Rush state. Predominately single men with a high rate of literacy and cosmopolitan attitudes, they too dreamed of staking their claim in the "Golden West." And they went at it just as energetically.

" 'Are they real Negroes?' I asked innocently and Jack said they were, down to the last drummer. And yet there was the familiar burnt cork. . . . Of course they opened with the spurious music which has come to be known as Negro melody. And it was only now and then that they drifted into the swinging rhythm which characterizes their own. 'What a curious thing it is,' observed Jack, after he had been thoroughly bored for some twenty minutes,—'[that] a white man makes a much better minstrel than a black man.' "

Betsy B.
Argonaut
May 6, 1882

"Nearly all of my successful songs have been based on the idea that I am getting the worst of it. I am 'The Jonah Man,' the man who, even if it rained soup, would be found with a fork in his hand and no spoon in sight."

Bert Williams
"The Comic Side of Trouble"
American Magazine
January 1918

BERT WILLIAMS AND GEORGE WALKER

The San Francisco Examiner *published "coon songs" from black musicals* (opposite and below) *on a regular basis—until the African American community staged a vigorous protest. The published song below is from* Clorindy, *a show written by the great African American poet Paul Laurence Dunbar with Will Marion Cook. Black composers were often forced by the conventions of the period to write in the style of white minstrelsy.*

Free and enslaved people of African descent were included in Spain's first expeditions to the western territories. The earliest San Francisco census, conducted in 1847, listed 10 blacks (9 men and a single woman) in a total population of 459. Later there were black cowboys, stagecoach drivers, gold miners, and cavalry regiments (known as "Buffalo Soldiers," because of their woolly hair) among the California trailblazers. And when the first non-Indian settlement was established in Los Angeles in 1871, 28 of its 44 inhabitants were African Americans.[1] In 1890 the black population of San Francisco hit a nineteenth-century peak of 1,847, roughly half of one percent of the total citizenry; Oakland had about the same ratio. Economic factors, including the expense of long-distance travel and employment discrimination, kept their numbers low.

But what the Bay Area's black settlers lacked in numbers they made up in resourcefulness. By 1870 there were two black schools, three black newspapers (two of which, the *Elevator* and the *Pacific Appeal,* demonstrated staying power), several black churches and benevolent societies, even annual African American balls and galas. Black citizens also organized politically to fight racist laws, holding the first annual State Convention of the Colored Citizens of California in 1855. A few became local celebrities, notably the mixed-race entrepreneur William Liedesdorff (owner of the city's first hotel and earliest steamboat company) and Mary Ellen "Mammy" Pleasant, a charismatic cook and boarding house manager who hobnobbed with the political elite.[2]

Despite their individual achievements, the collective progress of San Francisco's black residents and sojourners was thwarted by an insidious racism. Blacks could own land and businesses in California, slavery was never sanctioned, and the state stood with the Union during the Civil War. But before 1863 blacks were not allowed to testify against whites in a California trial; until 1870 they could not serve on juries; and schools were not truly desegregated until well into the next century. Their employment was generally limited to jobs in the maritime industry, menial labor, and railroad work. The newly powerful white-run unions kept San Francisco's blacks—and its much larger Chinese population—out of some occupations, and new tides of white residents periodically replaced them in others.

Local theaters did not exactly throw open their doors to people of color, either. When attending the larger playhouses, African Americans were automatically seated in the upper balcony—"nigger heaven," as it was cruelly and commonly known. As performers, they did not secure work in the first-run variety halls or second-rate theaters until the 1870s.

But blacks did appear onstage and in the audience in San Francisco long before then. Black dance halls existed from 1850; the most democratic in town, they also welcomed whites, Chinese, and Latinos. And occasionally some of the nitty-gritty saloons and melodeons of the Barbary Coast hired black singers, musical groups, and dancers to provide entertainment.[3]

Little documentation of the earliest black acts exist, since San Francisco newspapers usually did not record what went on in the "low class" halls. There's evidence of a black musical group regaling listeners at the Aquila de Ora gambling saloon in 1849; an observer described their act as "plaintive and moving."[4] And in his extensive research on the subject, Russell Hartley found that a nameless company of "Genuine Negro Minstrels" appeared with Lotta Crabtree at the Red Onion Opera House, probably in the mid-1850s.[5]

While black troubadors tried to scratch out a living, white minstrel groups were having a field day. San Francisco went minstrel-crazy in the 1850s and early 1860s. Fans of the form welcomed dozens of visiting troupes and helped launch the careers of such budding stars as the San Francisco Minstrels and Billy Emerson, considered one of the best all-around entertainers of his era.

Based extremely loosely on the music, dance, and speech patterns of black plantation slaves, minstrel shows were ritualized affairs mixing folksy political satire with sentimental songs, jigs, clog dances, and blackface travesties of operas and famous plays. Blacking themselves up gave white performers license to drop formalities and to play out their own fantasies of African American behavior in the guise of "funky darkies." The black mask permitted behavior that would have otherwise been socially unacceptable for whites—loud, crude, outlandish carrying-on that gave white audiences a vicarious thrill.

Sadly, the merriment came at the expense of African Americans. The minstrel charade spawned a bevy of such humiliating tunes as "All Coons Look Alike to Me" and "He's Just a Little Nigger, But He's Mine, All Mine." It also inspired weekly "coon songs" in the *San Francisco Examiner* and exaggerated cartoons depicting big-lipped, bulge-eyed blacks making vulgar, self-deprecating jokes in Deep South dialect.

This parade of ethnic stereotypes was a relentless assault on the

The last celebrated white "Ethiopian" minstrel was Billy Emerson, a superior singer and comedian. He first arrived in San Francisco in 1870 and did such great business for Tom Maguire that the producer helped him put together a very successful minstrel troupe under his own name. In 1877 he took over the Standard Theater, renamed it Emerson's Opera House, and there became one of the first "legit" managers to present African American and white variety artists on the same bill. This two-sided handbill (opposite) advertised one of his shows with ticket information on the front, stereotyped images of black southern life on the back.

dignity of black San Franciscans. In a letter to the *Pacific Appeal,* a reader complained about the nightly "Jim Crow Exhibitions and Extravaganzas" that exploited "the poverty and ignorance of an oppressed, long-outraged and downtrodden people." Of his fellow African Americans who perpetuated the stereotypes by becoming minstrels themselves, local poet James Madison Bell wrote, "This, Mr. Editor, is by far 'the unkindest cut of all.' "[6]

But in those days aspiring black entertainers had few options beyond minstrelsy. In San Francisco, some did appear as exotic specimens in side shows. Playbills trumpeted such acts as the "Aborigine Cannibals," "The Giant Black Man in Chains," and Millia Zoulouw, a "Dark Beauty and Snake Charmer." Evidence of other humiliations comes in an anecdote about a black carnival performer, reported gleefully in the *Wasp.* The writer describes a game at Woodward Gardens in which comers paid two bits to toss leather balls at the face of a "complaisant darkey, sitting with a roofless silk hat, partially concealed behind a wooden frame." As a prank, several professional baseball players took their turns, catching the black man "square between the eyes." He was "startled and astounded and the crowd roared. . . . The joke was all the more appreciated as a majority of the spectators had been previously sneered at by the now discomfited darkey when they tried and failed [to hit him]."[7]

Some African Americans fought for more elevated and refined performance careers. A few offered operatic and piano recitals in small halls, including a Mrs. Smith who sang at Mozart Hall in 1868. The influential concert dancer Juba and the great Shakespeare tragedian Ira Aldridge garnered high praise elsewhere, but never appeared in San Francisco. Both found more opportunities to perform in England than in the United States.

The most successful of the brave "high road" entertainers were the African American student chorales that flourished after the Civil War, touring the nation to raise money for emerging black colleges. One of the finest of these gospel choruses, the Fisk University Singers, concertized at the New Theater in San Francisco on January 3, 1876. That night a black patron, Charles Green, became so incensed at not being allowed to sit in the dress circle that he sued the manager for violation of his civil rights. Green lost his case on a technicality but succeeded in getting the New Theater to desegregate its seating anyway.[8]

There was no doubt that minstrelsy provided the major show business entrée for blacks: the best they could do was try to make the form their own and try to subvert self-ridicule into honest self-expression. When Sam Pride's Minstrels, one of the first black outfits, came to San Francisco in 1862, the *Pacific Appeal* critic was impressed enough to write in the April 19 issue, "We have witnessed the performance of this troupe and can speak favorably of their ability. . . . All who like to enjoy a good hearty laugh should go see them. There is nothing offensive or indelicate in their performances. Mr. Sam Pride is truly the Champion Banjoist of the World; he produces sounds from his banjo which we never thought an instrument so crude was capable of expressing."

In the 1870s a slew of other black minstrel troupes joined Pride's company on the road. San Francisco saw all of the best known—Haverly's Minstrels (who, remarkably, performed on one occasion with white minstrel Billy Emerson), the Cleveland Genuine Coloured Colossal Carnival Minstrels (James Bland, the composer of "Dem Golden Slippers" and "Carry Me Back to Old Virginny," was along for their 1889 run at the New Bush Theater), and the most popular of them all, the Callender Minstrels (also known as Callender's Georgia Minstrels). As the white minstrel fad died out, the fortunes of these dynamic black singers and comedians rose. At first they were viewed as novelties or, worse, as "nigger" interlopers out to defile the racial purity of the larger theaters. Later, as critics heaped praise on them, their race was accented in ads promising "genuine Negroes" or "real nigs," as opposed to white men in masquerade.

According to dance historian Marian Hannah Winter, the repertoires of these companies consisted mainly of "the sentimental ballad budget and music-hall jigs typical of all minstrel shows. The Negro element remained primarily in the rhythmic treatment of this material, the 'intangibles of performance,' and a phenomenal virtuosity in 'trick' dances."[9] Eventually blacks would make many more contributions to popular culture, but first they had to work within accepted parameters.

Blacks in minstrel audiences knew they were seeing practiced talent. But many whites believed black minstrels were *born* singers and dancers, or as historian Robert C. Toll put it, "they were thought of as natural, spontaneous people on exhibit rather than as professional entertainers."[10] Such misconceptions were exacerbated by the attitudes of condescending white manager-promoters like Charles Callender.

When Callender sensed the commercial potential of African American

Callender's Minstrels were among the first African American entertainers to appear before white audiences in major American theaters. They are pictured here in 1876.

minstrels, he formed a troupe made up of a cab driver (Sam Lewis), a
waiter (James Grace), a barber (Lew Brown), a bootblack (Billy Kersands),
and other men with no prior stage experience. He coached them in minstrel
techniques and taught them how to behave like "coons." In an interview
with a San Francisco journal, Callender took credit for his players' success
and granted them a begrudging compliment canceled out by an insult. "In
jubilee songs and plantation dances," he said, "[blacks] are superior to
white men and have the advantage of a natural dialect. But they have
scarcely any sense of humor."[11]

The New York–based Callender company came to the Standard
Theater in May 1882. It was a landmark event, probably the first time
blacks had headlined at a legitimate theater in San Francisco—and not just
any theater, but one recently managed by Billy Emerson. Response to the
show may be gauged by the perplexed notice from critic Betsy B. in the
Argonaut, in which Mrs. B's husband concludes that "a white man makes a
much better minstrel than a black man."[12] Later the same year, however,
the Callender crew were back again for David Belasco's Baldwin Theater
production of the southern drama *The Octoroon.* And in 1883 they returned
for a successful *Uncle Tom's Cabin* at the Grand Opera House.

Uncle Tom was a hot property for black and white entertainers alike.
Dramatic and minstrelized musical versions of the novel appeared soon
after Harriet Beecher Stowe published it in 1852, and it remained a
theatrical staple for over fifty years. Stowe's melodramatic exposé of
slavery added some unfortunate black stereotypes to our cultural lexicon,
and the major characters of Topsy, Tom, and Eliza were further exaggerated
onstage when blacked-up whites played them. Also, the story's original
antislavery message was often undercut by overwrought theatrics and
"happy pickaninny" musical numbers. But the "Tom" fad was, in its
mangled way, a step forward: it put more blacks onstage and eventually
allowed them to perform alongside whites.

In 1876 a San Francisco *Uncle Tom* advertised a "black Topsy" played
by the talented young actress Emma Grant. One critic hit the nail on the
head when he wrote that Grant "showed a great deal of talent, but to go
on the stage she would have to play Topsy all of her life. What an outlook
for her, and the public."[13] More commonly blacks appeared in the gimmicky
musical *Uncle Tom*s, like Callender's version and the one at the Orpheum
Theater in December 1888 with "two funny Topsys, 25 Plantation Singers, a

pack of imported bloodhounds, and Comical trick Donkeys."

Observing that blacks could go over big with white audiences, local producers began to hire more black performers for variety and musical shows—while still typecasting them as foreign exotics and grinning buffoons. In April 1892 the Orpheum presented *A Black Picnic* starring the Famous Criterions and "the renowned black comedian, Ernest Hogan," and (on another bill) *A Trip to Turkey!* with "the Black Nightingale, Mme Alberta." In 1893 a "spectacular comic opera" called *Africa!* did splendid business at the California Theater. It featured a silly libretto about explorers, coauthored by San Francisco's Clay M. Greene, and a dancing black chorus of "King Tippoo Tip's Attendants."

By the time Bert Williams met George Walker in 1893, the doors were inching open to black artists and about to swing wider. But a look at Williams's career in San Francisco and beyond illustrates how even the most successful black stage artists of the time met with frustration and humiliation as often as triumph and glory.

Born in the West Indies in 1874, raised by striving parents in Riverside, California (his father was a railroad porter), and educated briefly at Stanford University, Williams was an articulate, well-bred young man with no natural affinity for either the plantation drawl or the shuck-and-jive of minstrelsy. As a novice performer he tried to go another route, playing banjo tunes and telling jokes with a crew of students touring the Monterey area by wagon. He also headed up to the Humboldt County lumber camps with a ragtag variety troupe. Fending off boos and jeers, he even sang Irish ballads at the Hosker-Donken, Pat Ryan's Blue Shades, and other rowdy Barbary Coast saloons.

But Williams soon realized that if he wanted to perform for a living he had to "black up" and learn the mannerisms and dialect of the minstrels. Once he did, he found a between-acts singing gig at the San Francisco Museum, then a spot with an integrated ten-man troupe, Martin Seig's Mastodon Minstrels. When the Mastodons were one man short, Williams was sent out to find an end man. He came back with George Walker.

The two men made a striking pair, a perfect contrast for a double act. Williams was a shy, sensitive introvert; Walker was ebullient and gregarious, a self-confident Kansas native who had danced and sung his way west in medicine shows. Williams was light-skinned and stood over six feet tall; Walker was short and dark. What they had in common was strong racial

In 1906, George Walker (right) described his Market Street introduction to his partner Bert Williams: "While hanging around one day I saw a gaunt fellow over six feet, of orange hue and about 18 years of age, haggling with a manager—that was Bert A. Williams. He was stagestruck too! . . . That was fifteen years ago. We have had many ups and downs since those days, but we still hang together."

pride and abundant untapped talent.

After a brief stint with the Mastodons, the pair decided to strike out on their own. For nearly two years they found regular work as a team at the rough Midway Plaisance variety hall on Market Street. Eschewing burnt cork makeup and stereotypical costumes (flashy mock-evening wear or hobo tatters), they devised an act with Williams as straight man and banjo picker and Walker as comedian. In 1894 they also took on what must have been a galling job at the Midwinter Exposition in Golden Gate Park. When the "real savages" promised at the African Dahomian village exhibit were delayed en route, Walker and Williams were among the local black performers who donned animal skins to play "primitive."

The duo pushed on from San Francisco in 1895. Like many troupers, they had gained helpful experience in the city's saloons and small-time theaters. But the pay was abysmal and the overall prospects were grim. Variety performers, especially black ones, had to be on the go to survive.

Working their way across the country, Williams and Walker met with the psyche-scarring and life-threatening bigotry that was rampant at the time. In El Paso, Texas, where they were performing with a medicine show, a crowd hooting "uppity niggers" forced them to strip off their well-tailored stage clothes and don burlap sacks. After this ugly incident, Williams and Walker vowed never to play the South again, and they never did.[14]

Soon after, they took their act to more hospitable midwestern audiences and created the characters that would clinch their fame. Walker later recalled, "How to get before the public and prove what ability we might possess was a hard problem for us to solve. We thought that as there seemed to be a great demand for blackfaces on the stage, we would do all we could to get what we felt belonged to us by the laws of nature."[15] While Walker perfected the image of a flashy wise-guy who could do a mean strut and cakewalk, Williams blacked up again to impersonate a ragged, clumsy sadsack who, in the performer's own words, "was always getting the worst of it." This shuffling dunce delighted black and white audiences and proved a great conduit for Williams's tragicomedic flair.

But the pose was perilously close to minstrel caricature, the very thing Williams had tried so hard to avoid. And as Robert Toll has pointed out, the blackface mask that had been a boon to white minstrels "liberated Williams as an entertainer but . . . stifled him as a man." He became a black Pagliacci, a beloved clown on the outside and a melancholic within; W. C. Fields later described him as "the funniest man I ever saw and the saddest man I ever knew."[16]

Williams and Walker caught on like no other black act ever had, and their rise helped other African Americans make the transition from minstrelsy to vaudeville. In New York they played Tony Pastor's Music Hall and the other top variety halls, their renditions of the cakewalk (performed with Ada Overton Walker, George's talented wife) adding to the popularity of that black-generated dance craze. In 1899 they shifted from the vaudeville circuit to musical theater, starring in the tailor-made show *A Lucky Coon,* followed a couple of years later by their breakthrough smash *In Dahomey.* When the latter musical opened on Broadway in 1903, some wags feared a race war; none materialized and *Theatre Magazine* hailed Williams as "a vastly funnier man than any white comedian now on the stage." To further dignify the emerging class of professional African American entertainers, Williams and Walker helped form the Frogs, an early black theatrical association.

After a run of successes that included a command performance at England's Buckingham Palace and a triumphant return to San Francisco, Walker grew critically ill with advanced symptoms of syphilis; he died of the disease in 1911. But Williams continued to scale the heights. In 1910 he became the first black artist to appear in the *Ziegfeld Follies.* He expanded his repertoire of characters, drew warm praise from colleagues like Fields and Eddie Cantor, made more money per annum than the president of the United States, and became the first black superstar. But he still could not sleep in many hotels, nor enter certain public places by the front door, nor escape the tyranny of blackface makeup. When Williams died at forty-seven in 1922, his body weakened by years of hard drinking and overwork, the astute critic Heywood Broun wrote, "Bert Williams found prosperity and

success in the theater, but his high talents were largely wasted."[17]

The personal saga of Williams can be seen as a tragedy. But he and Walker did open the door for a wave of black performers who would fare better. At the end of the century the nation was still racially torn and fissured, yet there was no question that African Americans had taken the mainstage and were on it to stay.

In San Francisco this meant that the Orpheum Theater and the smaller Chutes frequently presented black acts on their vaudeville bills, including the beautiful operatic singer Sissieretta Jones (known as the "Black Patti") and her Colored Troubadours, as well as the Chocolate Dandies, the Funny Mitchells, the pianist Blind Tom, the integrated Primrose and West troupe, and many others. It meant a rage for early "Negro operas" including Will Marion Cook's Broadway hit *Clorindy*, which played the Orpheum in 1899, and the rousingly successful *Africa!* in 1893, with future dance great Pearl Inman in the cast. It meant the sounds of blues, syncopated ragtime, and nascent jazz in the Barbary Coast and Market Street cabarets and the cakewalk danced everywhere. In 1905, it meant the first San Francisco appearance of the brilliant dancer Bill "Bojangles" Robinson (the next black superstar) at the Orpheum, a smash 1906 San Francisco engagement of *In Dahomey* with Williams and Walker, and Williams's triumphant return as a solo act in 1911 with the *The Ziegfeld Follies* at the Columbia Theater.

One can look back at some of America's early black minstrels and accuse them of participating in the denigration of their own race, by their apparent willingness to wear the distorted comic mask others had created for them. That, however, would be both ungenerous and historically myopic. When a black college instructor castigated Bert Williams for failing to create positive images for black youth, Williams replied that he had been limited by the white audience's desire to see only "the antebellum 'darkey'" and by blacks' desire to see "such characters as to remind [them] of 'white folks'"—that is, white minstrels.[18]

Williams and the other black entertainers who broke the color barrier in San Francisco were indeed caught between a rock and a hard place. Their willingness to fight for their rightful position on the stage took real courage. And despite the initial limitations placed upon them as artists, they made distinctive, lasting contributions to a mainstream culture that long resisted their talents.

A turn-of-the-century vaudeville team, the Andersons appeared at the Orpheum and other large theaters catering primarily to a white clientele. Thanks to the doors opened by such pioneers as Williams and Walker, the Andersons were among the first African American artists to integrate mainstream show business. Offstage, however, black performers still found themselves barred from hotels, railroad cars, and eateries where their white colleagues were welcomed.

89

The Ol' Orph:
San Francisco Embraces Vaudeville

In Frank Norris's 1899 novel *McTeague,* a San Francisco dentist treats his lady friend Trina Sieppe, her mother, and her little brother to a night of vaudeville at the Orpheum Theater.

Dr. McTeague and his party entered the O'Farrell Street auditorium "absurdly" early, wrote Norris, and took their plush fourth row seats amidst white-aproned waiters who "hurried up and down the aisles, their trays laden with beer glasses." Once settled, the party "studied their programmes. First was an overture by the orchestra, after which came 'The Gleasons, in their mirth-moving musical farce, entitled "McMonnigal's Courtship." ' This was to be followed by 'The Lamont Sisters, Winnie and Violet, serio-comiques and skirt dancers.' And after this came a great array of other 'artists' and 'specialty performers,' musical wonders, acrobats, lightning artists, ventriloquists, and last of all, 'The feature of the evening, the crowning scientific achievement of the nineteenth century, the kinetoscope.' "

"McTeague was excited, dazzled," Norris continued. "In five years he had not been twice to the theatre. Now he beheld himself inviting his 'girl' and her mother to accompany him. He began to feel that he was a man of the world."[1]

This fictional account of an Orpheum outing (complete with made-up but entirely characteristic acts) captures the shape and dazzle of big-time nineteenth-century vaudeville and its allure for unsophisticated but upwardly mobile men like McTeague. As one analyst has observed, this potpourri of acts in garish surroundings enthralled newly citified folk "whom old-country folkways could no longer satisfy. . . . Vaudeville, which made a business of sensing their needs and catering to them, combined familiar rural and provincial symbols with those of the city and presented them in a program as fragmented as a novel and as varied as the urban experience itself."[2]

In the frenzied "Gay Nineties" of McTeague's San Francisco, vaudeville enthralled the masses, and the 3,500-seat Orpheum became the busiest, most accessible entertainment palace in town. A show went on every

"[Vaudeville] represents the almost universal longing for laughter, for melody, for color, for action, for wonder-provoking things. It exacts no intellectual activity on the part of those who gather to enjoy it; in its essence it is an enemy to responsibility, to worries, to all the little ills of life. It is joyously, frankly absurd, from the elemental nonsense of the funmakers to the marvelous acrobatic feats of performers who conceive immensely difficult things for the pleasure of doing them."

Hartley Davis
"In Vaudeville"
Everybody's Magazine
1905

91

THE ORIGINAL ORPHEUM THEATER, 1887–1906

Gustav Walter (below), *the self-named "director-general" of the Orpheum Theater, had managed numerous popular variety halls (the Fountain, Vienna Gardens, the Wigwam) before erecting the enormous Orpheum, the first West Coast version of the grand-scale vaudeville palaces Benjamin Keith was opening in the East. With vaudeville booming, Walter built two other Orpheums: one in Los Angeles, another in Sacramento. A large liquor debt soon forced the sale of his mini-empire to a group of managers led by Chicago impresario Martin Beck. It was Beck who parlayed the Orpheums into a smashingly successful seventeen-theater chain known as the Orpheum Circuit.*

night—rain or shine, depression or prosperity. The bills offered enough acts in an evening to satisfy the most gluttonous viewer, at an admission charge any humble workman or housewife could afford. The patrons were the lowly and the high-born, and the performers ranged from trick dog acts to the most celebrated opera and drama stars (when they could no longer resist the pay). The Orpheum was one of only three early vaudeville houses to import European artists, and by 1905 it reigned as the flagship house in the seventeen-theater chain known as the Orpheum Circuit.

The founder and self-designated "Director General" of the Orpheum was Gustav Walter, an immigrant German entrepreneur. Yet even before Walter opened the doors to his auditorium in 1887, other clever producers were ushering in San Francisco's vaudeville era—that is, they were putting on wholesome, respectable, marvel-laden entertainment for the "whole family," and they were franchising it around the country. (This was a change from variety, which tended to be bawdier and more regionalized.)

Among San Francisco's first vaudeville purveyors was Michael Leavitt. Born in West Prussia and raised in New England, Leavitt was a showman through and through. A child actor first, then an accomplished end man with the Hooley Minstrels and one of Tom Maguire's minstrel troupes, he soon seized on the more lucrative role of talent manager. In the 1870s he began handling touring variety and "girlie show" acts such as Leavitt's Gigantic Vaudeville Stars and Mabel Santley's English Burlesque Troupe—the risqué outfit that got him hauled into a San Francisco court on indecency charges in 1879, resulting in reams of free publicity for his "girls."

Though based in New York, Leavitt kept up a strong presence in San Francisco from 1882 to 1906 by controlling the Bush Street Theater (formerly known as the Alhambra and later the New Theater). Charles Locke, the house's previous manager, had booked in a variety of East Coast attractions, but he couldn't make them pay. Leavitt could, with practices that set the pattern for West Coast vaudeville and "combination" touring.

According to the *Chronicle*, in 1882 Leavitt had "over 175 performers, agents and musicians" under contract, making him one of the top talent managers in the country.[3] Forward-thinking and shrewd, he was an innovative tour profiteer who got his cut every step of the way. He did so by leasing or contracting with theaters from coast to coast, finagling discounted rail fares, and "owning" a percentage of all the talent he sent out in groups like M. B. Leavitt's All Star Specialty Company and Leavitt's

Gigantic Vaudeville Stars. (Al Hayman, one of Leavitt's early Bush Street assistants, elaborated on this scheme and in 1896 helped create the all-powerful Syndicate, whose complete domination of theatrical touring calls to mind another Frank Norris novel—*The Octopus,* an exposé of ruthless corporate monopolies.)

Leavitt kept the Bush Street supplied with attractions, though not just variety acts. He also presented popular farce units such as the Edward Harrigan Company and the Edouin Sparks Combination, and he brought in Minnie Maddern Fiske, Carrie Swain, Frank Mayo, the legendary Buffalo Bill, and other stars to appear in melodramas and light comedies. He had little artistic ambition: the only top drama troupe the Bush Street hosted was the esteemed Daly Stock Company.

Otherwise, the bills were mixed and matched according to prevailing middlebrow tastes, the surroundings were spiffy, the admission price was modest, the acts rode a circuit—virtually defining the fundamentals of wholesale vaudeville. Leavitt would later boast in his memoirs that the "new plan I had hatched completely changed the methods of the Western amusement," and that "these touring attractions sent by me across the continent . . . educated the San Franciscans to a higher class of vaudeville entertainment."[4]

The Orpheum adopted Leavitt's practices but applied them strictly to vaudeville. It was San Francisco's answer to the string of enormous vaudeville houses that the impresario Benjamin Franklin Keith began building on the East Coast in 1883. (The word "vaudeville," which Tony Pastor and Keith helped to popularize, comes from the term *vaux-de-Vire,* a French style of musical satire that dates back to the fifteenth century and has little relation to the American version.)

The Orpheum was not Gustav Walter's first show business endeavor, but it certainly was his most grand. Arriving in San Francisco from Germany in 1874, Walter worked as a bookkeeper until 1880, when he had enough cash to open The Fountain, a musical saloon on Kearny Street. He also managed the Vienna Gardens (a rival to the Tivoli) but really struck it rich operating the Wigwam Variety Hall, a popular theater that interspersed opera segments with other fare.

In 1886 Walter bankrolled construction of the Orpheum Theater (also called the Orpheum Opera House). Built specifically as a showcase for vaudeville, the mammoth, well-appointed structure became the largest hall

Herr Grais put on one of the many well-received animal acts at the Orpheum. Animal routines—involving dogs, birds, monkeys, rabbits, donkeys, horses, even chickens—were very popular in early vaudeville, despite the potential for well-rehearsed routines to go awry.

The singing and dancing Four Cohans, including young George M. Cohan (at left), exerted great appeal at the Orpheum. From a tender age, George traveled the national vaudeville circuit with his father Jerry, mother Helen, and sister Josephine. Eventually he wrote skits for the clan. In 1904, the twenty-six-year-old entertainer attracted much attention in his flag-waving musical Johnny Jones, which featured his own peppy renditions of "Give My Regards to Broadway" and "The Yankee Doodle Boy." Soon Cohan was a Broadway fixture, the author-songwriter-director-star of more than a dozen shows that were unabashedly chauvinistic and sentimental, and undeniably popular with the public.

in San Francisco when it opened with fanfare on June 30, 1887. The boxes bore gilt scrolling and the stage curtain was an elaborate affair depicting swans, marble vases, and a gondola. Yet ticket prices were low: ten cents for children anywhere and adults in the balcony, twenty-five cents for reserved adult orchestra tickets, fifty cents to sit in the boxes.

The Orpheum's first headliner was Rosner's Electric Orchestra from Budapest, Hungary, which shared the bill with a troupe of high-flying aerialists and a clutch of other acts from Europe and the East Coast. Rosner had a great gimmick: a symphony of electrically-run instruments that played themselves at the stroke of his baton. The whole shebang cost a pricey $6,500 to import. The public responded warmly to the new venue and kept Rosner's musical novelty in town for six months.

Walter truly loved music, and he employed the well-qualified Adolph Bauer as the Orpheum's initial conductor. For the first several years Walter occasionally inserted into the Orpheum schedule full-fledged operas by such large touring troupes as the C. D. Hess Grand Opera Company and the Columbia Opera Company (which introduced San Francisco to Mascagni's *Cavalleria Rusticana*). He also harkened back to his Vienna Gardens days by bringing in Erz-Herzog Joseph's Gypsy Band to play "strange, weird, half savage, but wholly musical czardas of the Hungarian peasantry."[5]

Eventually the Orpheum devoted itself exclusively to the eclectic best in vaudeville—definitely the people's choice. And to scout talent from the East and Europe, Walter opened his own booking agency in New York, a bold and productive maneuver at the time. The burlesque sketch team of Weber and Fields (part of a new wave of ethnic humorists), the dancing and singing Four Cohans (including the young George M.), the remarkable magician Harry Houdini, Sissieretta Jones, the boy acrobat Charles Chaplin, the "belle of the Nineties" Lillian Russell, the great Papinta and her volcano dance, the endearing comic actress Marie Dressler, the renowned impersonator Riviere—they were among the scores of then-illustrious performers to hold forth on the Orpheum stage.

A glowing item in the *Call* suggests the excitement that the theater could generate: "The Orpheum has been crowded every night during the past week. . . . Manager Walter announces seven new people for this week's programme. Some of the performers come direct from Paris and the remainder from New York City. On the new list are Mazuz and Abacco, acrobatic comedians; Lind and Vani, an eccentric comedy duo; the Nawns, Irish character artists, and Kalkasa, a celebrated comic juggler. The new people come highly recommended and the management draws special attention to the programme as being one of the strongest yet presented. Indeed, the high standard of the attractions at the Orpheum for the past year has made it difficult to secure stronger features from the entire vaudeville world than those which have already been presented."[6]

Gelett Burgess, a *Lark* correspondent who haunted the Orpheum in search of beautiful young vaudevillians to interview, found the audience as stimulating as the show folk. The Orpheum, he wrote, "is a dull, smoky, colorless hall, with a single gallery, and it is frequented by the most varied audience in the world. Here assemble men-about-town, gamblers, debutantes, mothers-of-families, mondaines [prostitutes] and demi-dittos, black-legs, touts, Chinamen, Italian fishermen, bankers, princes, and tourists of all descriptions. I might, in fact, have got as interesting interviews in front of the footlights as behind."[7]

Vaudeville headliner Papinta created striking theatrical effects with mirrors and light, costumes and music. Known especially for an eruptive novelty number billed as her "volcano dance," she toured successfully throughout the world and settled eventually on a 162-acre horse ranch near Concord.

Though it lacked the elegance of the Grand Opera House and the high society tone of the Baldwin, the Orpheum was just as much a place to see and be seen. In her book *Champagne Days of San Francisco,* Evelyn Wells imagines a California senator's sybaritic Sunday on the town in the 1890s. The lawmaker begins by breakfasting at Colonel Dickey's cafe with a judge and other pals, later escorts his wife to an exhibit of art in the old Mark Hopkins mansion, wolfs down a simple ten-course dinner, and hightails it to the Orpheum, where he flirts with the captivating blonde "Queen of the Underworld" Bessie Hall while listening to comedian Will Fox send-up "Padewhiskie" (Paderewski) at the piano. (Hall did exist, and every Sunday night she brought her retinue of "beauties" to the Orpheum; Fox, too, was for real.) After a long, amusing show, and a pit stop at Doctor Zeile's steam baths on Pacific Street, the senator toddled home to his Nob Hill manse in the wee hours.[8]

Flush with success, Gustav Walter established a second Orpheum in Los Angeles in 1894 and a third in Sacramento soon after. But he ran into trouble over an unpaid $50,000 liquor bill and was forced to surrender his mini-empire to a group of managers that included the sly midwestern impresario Martin Beck. Beck also went for class: he booked Sarah

Bernhardt at $7,000 a week (a record salary for the time) and reeled in other stars. A marketing genius who deftly juggled highbrow and lowbrow attractions, Beck extended the Orpheum Circuit all the way to Chicago. He migrated East, eventually to build the grandest vaudeville shrine of them all: Broadway's Palace Theater.

As the Orpheum thrived, so did San Francisco vaudeville across the board. A more humble theater dedicated to the form sprang up in 1895. Located on Haight between Clayton and Cole streets, the Chutes Theater was originally part of an amusement park named for its thrilling "shoot the chutes" ride—a boat trip over a cascading waterway and into a manmade lake. There and in several other locations, the Chutes was never half so impressive as the Orpheum. But it had a big following for the likes of Nora Bayes (who introduced the song "Shine on Harvest Moon"), Eddie Cantor, Al Jolson, Sophie Tucker, and other emerging stars.

Dora Barrett, a San Francisco child star in variety and vaudeville who went by the stage name "Baby Dody," recalled the "spellbinding" delights of the Chutes and the glories of the Orpheum. She also noted the camaraderie of the itinerant vaudevillians who lived out of trunks and played up to three shows a day. "In spite of their transiency," Barrett

Vaudeville duos from the tenth anniversary program of the Orpheum Theater: the Kronemanns, Conway and Leland, the Vaidis Sisters, and, in a different act, Conway and Leland.

*Many legendary American comic per-
formers started out in vaudeville ,
including W. C. Fields, Marie Dressler, Bert Williams, and the Marx
Brothers, to name just a few. Among
the early favorites on the Orpheum
Circuit was Nat Wills, known (and
pictured here) as "The Happy Tramp."
Apparently, Wills's offstage life was
none too happy: bankrupted by high
alimony payments and the constant
acquisition of expensive new material
for his act, he committed suicide in
1917 at the zenith of his popularity.*

The Happy Tramp,

NAT M. WILLS

COMING TO THE *Orpheum* NEXT WEEK

wrote, "[they] knew each other or of each other. There was a code of
loyalty among them. . . . Dressing room walls were bulletin boards . . .
that left all sorts of pertinent information for travelling vaudevillians—an
unpleasant situation at a local hotel, unfair prices, forewarnings of un-
desireable [sic] business, or perhaps a personal message for a friend."[9]

Of all the vaudeville and variety houses that existed in San Francisco,
only the Orpheum survives today in any form—actually, in its fifth
incarnation. The 1906 earthquake gutted the first Orpheum. Soon after, the
management set up shop in the still-standing Chutes—at the time located
on Fulton Street, between Tenth and Eleventh avenues. In 1907 a third
Orpheum rose up on Ellis Street near Fillmore on the assumption that the
Fillmore District would become the heart of the rebuilt city. But by 1909
the old Market Street downtown had been resurrected, triggering the
construction of yet another Orpheum on O'Farrell between Stockton and
Powell.

The fifth and final Orpheum, on the corner of Market and Hyde
streets, was built as the New Pantages for the national Pantages chain. It
was acquired in 1929 by R.K.O. (Radio-Keith-Orpheum), a mammoth
conglomerate that would soon convert most of the Orpheum chain into
movie houses. Fire destroyed the Orpheum on O'Farrell in 1975, but the
historic Market Street venue has endured. It evolved from a movie house to
the home of the San Francisco Civic Light Opera to its current identity as
one of several Broadway touring houses managed by local producer Carole
Shorenstein Hays.

Little remains of Orpheum-style vaudeville itself. It was eventually
eclipsed by and absorbed into more profitable kinds of mass entertainment:
movies, radio, and finally television. Now and then a nostalgic revival of
the form like *Hellzapoppin'* or *Sugar Babies* turns up on Broadway. And
the "New Vaudeville" movement, which blossomed in San Francisco during
the 1970s and 1980s, drew some inspiration from the spirit (if not the form)
of old vaudeville.

Nonetheless, vaudeville had lasting impact on the American cultural
scheme. It catalyzed and responded to a demand for the kind of escapist,
fast-moving, eclectic fare that now dominates the live and electronic media.
It schooled some of the twentieth century's finest performers, from the
Marx Brothers to Fred Astaire. And it proved that there was a vast
commercial market for such diversions and that San Francisco was a key

segment of that market.

Not everyone in San Francisco heralded the shift toward high-volume, mass-market show biz when they first saw it coming, because it came at a price. As vaudeville boomed, the city lost its best dramatic venues. The New California Theater gave up on classic dramas performed by thespians of the old school and in the 1890s went over to second-rate drama troupes and vaudeville bills. The Baldwin Theater, handsomely renovated in 1888 to host such important events as the local premiere of Henrik Ibsen's landmark drama of realism, *A Doll's House,* perished in a 1898 fire and was not rebuilt. The Alcazar thrived, but usually with formulaic material.

Soon, only the Columbia Theater (formerly Stockwell's) was committed to top-drawer touring drama, largely because it was controlled by the Theatrical Syndicate—which also controlled nearly all the stars and plays of merit routed out of New York. And not all of these shows excited the blood, arriving (as they often did) shopworn and carelessly cast after several years on the road.

San Francisco critics who remembered the transcendent power of Booth and McCullough, Barrett and Modjeska, didn't exactly kick up their heels for vaudeville. In 1897 the *Wasp*'s "First Nighter" commented, "For fifteen years past the American stage has steadily declined in merit. It has been overrun by wretched combinations of barnstorming fakirs, who knew not the rudiments of the art trespassed."[10]

The *Chronicle*'s Peter Robertson, the *eminence grise* of San Francisco theater criticism, blamed the shift to vaudeville on a decline in literary drama: "Why do the variety houses pay?" he wrote in 1896. "Because just at present they offer more enjoyable entertainment. . . . Nearly every kind of play seems to have been run into the ground. Comedies are silly or weak; society plays are stupid or hackneyed; and musical comedy of late has neither wit nor music to keep life in it."[11] A decade later, reminiscing about the city's bygone glory years of drama, Robertson lamented, "Indeed, we don't seem to have any place a man of real taste can go regularly. The theatrical business today is merely one of hot cross buns."[12]

Those hot cross buns went over well, though, especially when dusted with the sugar and spice that vaudeville liberally sprinkled on. And at the Orpheum, a dime or a quarter virtually guaranteed what many folks were hankering for: an inexpensive night on the town in a temple of magic, hokum, and surefire delight.

Sissieretta Jones, a thrilling operatic soprano also known as "Black Patti," was one of vaudeville's first African American stars. She drew accolades whenever she appeared at the Orpheum with her Colored Troubadours, in revues that stressed her virtuosic singing and her company's athletic displays of "Negro dancing." Jones was a tireless trouper who clocked in over 2,400 performances in eight years. In addition to her erstwhile touring, she starred in a long-running New York revue at Proctor's 58th Street Theater.

Entertainment Alfresco:
The Lure of the Open Air

If you stood in the middle of the downtown theater district during the late 1800s, San Francisco didn't look so much different from a dozen other bustling American cities. Streets clotted with traffic, dense rows of tall and squat brick and wooden buildings, road dust and coal smoke clouding the air—such was the urban ambience.

But a parallel San Francisco existed as well, an oasis of panoramic vistas and virgin Pacific beaches, burnished sunlight and wine-hued sunsets, fog-crowned hills and craggy cliffs. This was the "flashing and golden pageant of California" that the poet Walt Whitman described with awe in his poem "Song of the Redwood-Tree" from *Leaves of Grass*. This was the gateway to the windswept, verdant, redwood-blessed Northern California that poets and philosophers posed as a new Mediterranean utopia, a citadel (in historian Kevin Starr's words) "of nature and art" where life could be "lived with dignity and celebrated in creativity."[1]

Not all San Franciscans shared those lofty ideals. But the temperate climate and topographical wonders of the region certainly did affect the way life was lived in the city, contributing to its general enthusiasm for open-air performances. In many cases, performing outdoors was a conscious, ritualized effort to commune with the physical and spiritual grandeur of the natural environment and to celebrate its cosmic essence.

Most of the town's early alfresco entertainments, however, were informal and convivial affairs, circus-style shows or California adaptations of what went on in European beer gardens and amusement parks. The outdoor "resorts" that thrived in the 1850s to the 1870s were privately-owned spreads of lawn and flora, islands of nature in a city that had not yet given much attention to creating municipal parks. (San Francisco's Golden Gate Park, one of the most ambitious urban parks ever conceived, wasn't completed until 1893.)

Russ Gardens, the first of the local resorts, opened in 1853 and became a favored spot for picnics, athletic events, and such nationalistic celebrations as Bastille Day and the Fourth of July. The Willows, a peppy

"Lo! here sit we mid the sun-
   down seas
   And the white sierras. The swift,
   sweet breeze
Is about us here; and the sky so fair
   Is bending above in its azaline
   hue,
   That you gaze and you gaze in
   delight, and you
See God and the portals of heaven
   there."

Joaquin Miller
In San Francisco, 1889

"One must have spent long days and nights in the mountains of northern California beneath the giant trees that have covered the hills for centuries. . . . One must have forded the rushing rivers, and trodden the mountain trails at dawn, in the glory of 'sunful-eyed noon,' at twilight, and in the dark fragrance of midnight. We had a camp there which was an Arden in an Arcady. We were all young, happy and sane beneath those boughs, and there came to us there a revelation of simple living, and clean-minded pastimes. To the town, variegated in its colour, so shut off from many of the tyrannies of the world, we brought back some of the impulses of the hills, and with those primal emotions were mingled many subtler reactions which no civilized being can do without."

Gelett Burgess
Bayside Bohemia, 1954

ANNUAL BOHEMIAN CLUB PLAY, MUIR WOODS, 1892

A nineteenth-century precursor to Disneyland, the amazing Woodward's Gardens featured a zoo, floral displays, an aquarium, an art gallery, a large amphitheater for musical and dramatic entertainment, and many other attractions—including freak shows. Eventually the charms of Woodward's were replaced by the lure of a great new outdoor playground: Golden Gate Park.

Mission Street outpost constructed in 1857, added entertainment to the landscape. In addition to vine-covered grottoes, a horseracing track, shooting galleries, and a small menagerie, the Willows boasted an open-air stage where the young Lotta Crabtree, the McClellan Brass Band, minstrel Johnny DeAngelis, and other well known artists cavorted. The place offered a congenial, wholesome alternative to the Barbary Coast melodeons until 1864, when the twin scourges of fire and flood destroyed it.

Two years later an Irish-American entrepreneur named Thomas Hayes opened Hayes Park on his 150-acre parcel (now Hayes Valley), gracing it with a pavilion that the city directory described as an "elegant resort" and "a prominent and imposing structure, three stories in height."[2] To keep his many visitors amused, Hayes hired romantic balladeers and brass bands, and he presented fairytale ballets by ensembles like the popular Martinettis. He also scheduled balloon ascensions and daring (but unsuccessful) launches of "aerial flying machines."

But the most successful San Franciscan in the outdoor amusement business was Robert Woodward. This noted hotelier and obsessive collector turned the grounds of his Mission District mansion (and later the mansion itself) into Woodward's Gardens, a magnet for San Francisco's growing population of families. At its zenith in the 1870s, Woodward's establishment accommodated up to fifteen thousand customers a day and answered many recreational needs at one go. The block-long establishment boasted a Museum of Natural Wonders (crystals, petrified animals, precious stones), an art gallery stocked with European paintings and sculptures, the largest zoo on the West Coast, and the nation's first saltwater aquarium.

There was an amphitheater too, of course, where patrons took in trendy attractions of the day: Gilbert and Sullivan's *HMS Pinafore*, Yankee Robinson's "Ballet of Parisian Beauties," and the antics of Haverly's Mastodon Minstrels. But Woodward, who had a streak of the carny in him, also presented such "exhibits" as a two-headed child, a man with no legs, and a headless rooster. As the *Examiner* archly reported, "any freak that didn't make [P. T.] Barnum gasp Woodward seized on with avidity."[3]

Singers, minstrels, and circus oddities helped draw the throngs into Woodward's Gardens, as did the fresh air, manicured gardens, and flowering trees. But the stage fare had little (if anything) to do with the sylvan setting. It was just an assortment of indoor theater acts, transplanted outdoors. By contrast, the San Francisco aesthetes who invented the

Bohemian Grove drama revered nature and sought a dynamic interaction with it. Their motives in creating drama among the redwoods were fiercely noncommercial. In fact, the Grove plays have always received elite private performances, never open to the public.

The long-enduring Bohemian Grove play is a uniquely San Francisco phenomenon, a hybrid of nature worship and hedonism, conservationism and male bonding, romantic poetry and pagan drama. Over time this ritual became the central ceremony of the Bohemian Club, a fraternal order founded by a group of San Francisco journalists and printers in 1872 that exists to this day.

The club was inspired in part by the nineteenth-century European *vie bohème* movement, which recast artists from worker-artisans into free-spirited iconoclasts and enemies of bourgeois convention. A more immediate catalyst was Gold Rush author Bret Harte's half-jesting call for a new order of California bohemianism. "Bohemia has never been located geographically," Harte wrote in 1860, "but any clear day when the sun is going down, if you mount Telegraph Hill, you shall see its pleasant valleys and cloud-capped hills glittering in the West."[4]

Choosing "Weaving Spiders Come Not Here" as their motto and the owl as their symbol, the first members of the Bohemian Club rented rooms in the Astor House on Sacramento Street, then recruited other like-minded men as fellow members. Among their ranks were such creative notables as writer-economist Henry George, cartoonist Jules Tavernier, writer Ambrose Bierce, poet George Sterling, and critic-playwright Peter Robertson. Naturalist John Muir (founder of the Sierra Club) joined up too, as did prominent businessmen and military officers. (Theirs, presumably, was a very respectable sort of bohemianism.) Former San Francisco scribes Bret Harte and Mark Twain held honorary membership, and the club prided itself on feting such visiting (male) wordsmiths as Oscar Wilde, Rudyard Kipling, and Robert Louis Stevenson.

What most distinguished the Bohemian Club from other bastions of male privilege were its paganistic leanings and flair for high drama. The group's first theatrical activity was the "Jinks," a weekly salon that began meeting in 1874. The salon had two components: the high-minded "High Jinks" followed by the frisky "Low Jinks." In the "High Jinks," members read poems and papers aloud, performed music, displayed paintings and drawings—all, notes scholar Joanne Lafler, "upon a theme proposed in

Bret Harte was a prominent literary figure in San Francisco's Gold Rush days. A journalist and fiction author, he served as the editor of the prestigious Overland Monthly *and was a frequent contributor to the* Golden Era. *At one point, Harte issued a half-jesting call for a new order of California bohemianism, in which artists and writers would fashion themselves as nature-worshiping iconoclasts. Though he migrated East in 1870, the founders of the Bohemian Club later made good on Harte's suggestion—and repaid him with an honorary membership in their elite new all-male society.*

advance by the Sire, as the master of ceremonies was called." The theme could be a tribute to Shakespeare, Dickens, or some other literary great, or it could treat an abstract subject such as "Wit, Wisdom, and Wickedness." (Once a year there was a "Ladies' Jinks," "the only occasion for which women were admitted to the clubrooms.") After the "High Jinks"—and a break for copious servings of food and drink—came the "Low Jinks," an extemporaneous session of wit-sparring.[5]

A new ritual was added in the late 1870s when the club instituted annual midsummer encampments in the redwoods north of San Francisco—a sort of Dionysian summer camp for grown-up males that Robert Bly might have dreamed up. During the 1880 camp-out the "High Jinks" ended with a brand-new custom: a mock-funeral and the cremation of an effigy of "Care," a symbol of the pressures and responsibilities the Bohemians hoped to escape at their bucolic retreats. The Cremation of Care was such a hit that it was repeated annually, growing ever more elaborate each year. Chanting choruses, an oration by a "high priest," and fireworks displays were added. All was solemn until the rockets exploded; after that, drinking and merrymaking ensued.

Over the years this ceremony evolved in a more mystical and theatrical direction, drawing on an eclectic array of religious, literary, and pop-cultural influences. In 1892 at Muir Woods, the participants performed beneath a seventy-foot statue of Buddha. The next year the event had a Druid theme and took place in a two-thousand-acre redwood grove by the Russian River, which became the club's permanent summer site. In 1894, with Peter Robertson as Sire, a stage was erected in the grove for the "Gypsy Jinks," a loosely constructed drama about unfettered gypsies triumphing over Care.[6]

The stage remained. And by 1902, the first fully scripted, plotted, directed, and rehearsed Grove Play appeared on it. Titled (aptly) *The Man in the Forest*, it featured a text by Charles K. Field, music by Joseph D. Redding, and a story about a noble white man who stumbles onto a sacred wood occupied by Native Americans and—what else?—banishes the destructive spirit of Care from their midst.

From then on a new version of the Grove Play was written, composed, and presented by Bohemian Club members nearly every year: *Montezuma, Saint Patrick at Tara, The Green Knight,* to name a few. The pageantry multiplied, encompassing larger casts, bigger orchestras, and more detailed

Some members of the Bohemian Club gather for a portrait, circa 1886..

costumes. The plots, characters, and titles changed every summer. But the central mythology remained constant: the idealization of the natural world and the Dionysian impulse, the pantheistic references and rites, the vanquishing of Care, the slapstick sequences and inside jokes, and a certain aura of mystery. Describing *Hamadryads*, the 1904 Grove play authored by Will Irwin, photographer Arnold Genthe remarked, "Such was the spell cast by the text of the play, the acting, the lighting, and the cathedral forest, that it was as if a long lost dream had been given a reality."[7]

The Grove Play is one of California's most durable dramatic traditions; a fresh version is still staged in the Bohemian Grove every summer, by and for male club members and their (male) guests. The play format remains the same, but the membership of the organization and its general tone are greatly changed. It is ironic that the idealistic Bohemian Club founders, though certainly not social drop-outs, held some of the same romantic attitudes and ideals championed in the 1960s by the hippies of Northern California. In contrast, today's club members are primarily business executives and politicians, the nation's rich, powerful, and politically conservative elite. The summer encampments have evolved into raucous networking sessions, with governmental heads (former President Richard Nixon among them) and corporate honchos (the chief officers of Bechtel Corporation) as featured speakers.

The club's ironic transformation from a circle of literary-minded, romantic iconoclasts to a fraternity for the wealthy and influential is underscored each year by the pickets outside the summer encampment. Anti–Vietnam War protestors, feminist groups, and homeless advocates have picketed the Grove, and in 1971 Sonoma County sheriffs raided the summer meeting to flush out prostitutes. Even so, the Bohemian Club and its theatrical tradition endure.

In 1903, the Northern California dream of celebrating art in the open air took a more democratic and accessible form in the construction of the Greek Theater in the Berkeley hills. The benefactor of this massive stone amphitheater was no dreamy poet but the philanthropist king of "yellow journalism," *San Francisco Examiner* publisher William Randolph Hearst. The theater was designed by Julia Morgan, a pioneering woman architect who was also responsible for the Hearst Castle in San Simeon and for many other distinctive California structures.

Residents of Berkeley, home of the conservationist Sierra Club

The annual Grove Play, usually an elaborately staged mythological pageant celebrating the vanquishing of the spirit of Care, is still performed today at the club's private Sonoma County encampment. This photo records one of the play's early incarnations.

The Greek Theater at the University of California at Berkeley was paid for by San Francisco Examiner *publisher William Randolph Hearst and designed by Julia Morgan, the pioneering woman architect also responsible for the Hearst Castle in San Simeon and many distinctive Bay Area homes and public structures. This massive stone arena, built to the specifications of the ancient outdoor drama setting at Epidaurus, Greece, was the most impressive of numerous Hellenistic amphitheaters built in California in the early 1900s.*

(founded in 1892) and the esteemed University of California at Berkeley, had begun to consider their small city an Athens of the West too. The creators of the Greek Theater took this Hellenistic metaphor literally, adapting their design from that of the classic dramatic arena at Epidaurus. It is proportioned accordingly: the massive stage measures 130 feet long by 28 feet deep. The back wall, flanked by Doric columns, stands 42 feet high. The tiered stone benches accommodate nearly eight thousand people.[8]

If the amphitheater itself was imposing, so was its location. The structure occupied a hillside stretch of the University of California campus—a western-facing slope open to azure skies and blazing afternoon sun. As it turned out, the amphitheater was also vulnerable to the penetrating wind and thick, wet fog that sometimes rolled in unbidden. (One Greek Theater production of *The Trojan Women* was nicknamed, aptly, *The Frozen Women*.)[9]

In keeping with the Grecian motif, the first performance in the amphitheater was Aristophanes' *The Birds*. But later productions eschewed Hellenic simplicity for the fussy scenic "realism" that was in vogue at the time. A British company lugged real trees onstage to foliate its version of *A Midsummmmer Night's Dream*. And when New York producer Charles Frohman brought in a company headed by former San Franciscan Maud Allan to play *As You Like It*, he insisted on covering the stately Grecian columns with a "sky" of blue bunting.[10]

The Greek Theater continued on at first as a venue for other leading drama companies and actors, including Sarah Bernhardt. Its fame also inspired the construction of several smaller scale classic amphitheaters in other areas of California. But theatrical styles have changed. Few classic dramas are performed there now, and in the past several decades the Greek Theater has most often presented musical events, including rock, folk, and jazz festivals.

The Greek Theater did not inspire the "returning of the drama to the people's hands as a religious force" hoped for by California visionaries like writer Mary Austin. But no matter what style of performance it accommodates, it remains a monument to the desire of many Northern Californians to recapture the Mediterranean wedding of art and nature— and, as Austin phrased it, to find "a new and more consoling expression of man's relation to the invisible."[11]

Fairy Queens, Chorines & Free Spirits: Women Change the Dance

Fairy queens in flouncy tutus twirled through enchanted forests. Sinuous figures draped in lace mantillas tapped out Spanish rhythms to the clickety-clack of castanets. Lines of voluptuous chorines kicked their ample legs in unison. Minstrels jigged, clogged, and cakewalked.

Dance was ubiquitous on San Francisco stages of the late nineteenth century. No musical play, no vaudeville revue, no opera production was complete without it. And offstage, the dance halls teemed with fun-loving men and women trying out the latest in fancy footwork.

But as the century turned, some new moves were afoot, born of dance impulses very different from the borrowed traditions of European ballet and the crowd-pleasing adaptations of folk and social dances. In the prime breeding ground of California, a new kind of dance expression was gestating. It was elemental yet abstract, ancient yet contemporary, strongly influenced by distant epochs and cultures but unmistakably American in temperament. Just as the decadent excesses of romantic painting and music would soon be challenged by modernist art and avant-garde musical composition, so would American dance react against the rigid formality of European classical ballet and the hammy frivolity of show-stepping.

In the late 1800s, before this revolution was in full swing, social and saloon dancing in San Francisco were dismissed as *déclassé*, and theatrical dance was rarely taken seriously as art. Whether they performed the cancan in a Barbary Coast cabaret or frolicked as fairies at the Grand Opera House, female dancers were still considered just a shade more respectable than prostitutes.

There were, of course, exceptions, dancers who won San Francisco's esteem in the best theaters with their grace, beauty, and (most of all) their European credentials. In the Gold Rush days, *La Sylphide* was performed to good reception by the French ballerinas Mme Celeste and Aurelia Dimier and visiting troupes like the Monplaisirs. And in 1853 the Rousset sisters starred in the San Francisco debut of *Giselle*.[1] During the 1870s such famous Italian ballerinas as Marie Bonfanti, Euphrosyne Parepa-Rosa, and La Rita Sangalli appeared locally to very positive response. In 1890 the

109

ISADORA DUNCAN, CIRCA 1893

Mme Celeste (below) and Mlle Cornalba (right) were two of the numerous European ballerinas who impressed San Francisco with their grace, beauty, and almost mechanistic skill in the years following the Gold Rush. Quite often, however, such terpsichorean stars would be backed up by an amateurish corps de ballet of local girls, who had little access to the kind of rigorous training European dancers received at La Scala or Covent Garden. Dance was gradually becoming more acceptable to Puritan America, but the country still lacked high-caliber dance conservatories and native professional ballet companies.

premier German *danseuse* Fraulein Clara Qualitz and the "Flying Dancer" Azilla won raves in a fairy tale ballet, *The Crystal Slipper.*[2]

But the term "ballet" was much more elastic a century ago than it is today. It was applied in America not only to the refined, airborne dance style that is now synonymous with classical ballet, but also to displays of theatrical acrobatics, saucy burlesque dancing by "leg troupes" like the Zavistowski Sisters and Lydia Thompson's British Blondes, and garish dance extravaganzas that were extensions of England's pantos (pantomimes) and Italy's opera-theater spectacles.

For cultural and religious reasons, it was a long time before dance as an art form took hold in the United States. Back in the 1700s, while the French and Germans were developing their great ballet traditions, the Puritans were frowning on dance as devil's play. By the late 1800s dance was much more acceptable in the United States, but there were still no permanent classical dance companies or high-caliber dance conservatories. That made for lax performance standards. On the San Francisco stage, European ballerinas rigorously trained at Covent Garden, La Scala, and the Paris Opera would routinely be supported by ragged *corps de ballet* of enthusiastic but ill-prepared local girls.

Even when the dancing was of a consistently high quality, it tended to be jumbled up with the other forms of light entertainment that San Franciscans loved. Consider the Martinettis, probably California's first resident "dance" company. Originally from France, the Martinetti clan toured the West in the 1850s in the company of their celebrated teacher, Gabriel Ravel. In 1860 they returned to San Francisco to form their own troupe with members of the Lehman family. *La Sylphide* was in their repertoire, but they mostly produced frothy, acrobatic fairy tales, including such favorites as *The Green Monster, The Magic Trumpet, The Red Gnome,* and *Raoul, or The Magic Star.*

In 1861, after a very successful first season in San Francisco, the Martinettis bought a thousand-seat tent and nine covered wagons and struck out on a pioneering Western states dance tour. Not everyone approved of the tent. Scoffed one critic, "In such a den, posturing and horse-drama are at home; but not the so-called High Art of French ballet-dancing, at least, after having been so long used to it in a comfortable and beautiful theater."[3]

But the Martinettis were not purists about the "so-called High Art of

Mlle.
Conalba

Hailing from Hungary, Bolossy and Imre Kiralfy were dancers and acrobats who began producing their own spectacular stage shows in 1874. For the next fifteen years they enjoyed success after success on Broadway, mounting and eventually touring such lavish theme musicals as Azurine, Antiope, and later (for the Barnum & Bailey Circus) megaproduction numbers such as Columbus and the Discovery of America, dubbed a "sublime nautical, martial and poetical spectacle." San Francisco was always a great market for this sort of extravaganza.

French ballet-dancing." No local papers employed dance critics yet, and drama reviewers rarely gave detailed descriptions of the actual choreography they witnessed. But the Martinettis' reviews do strongly suggest that the troupe put more emphasis on fanciful costumes and sets, gestural acting with a mimetic and *commedia* flavor, and acrobatic stunts like tumbling and wire-walking than on extended passages of pure movement. In January 1867 the *Bulletin* described their *Italian Brigands* as "a series of illuminated Tableaux," and concluded that all the company's "pantomime and lighter pieces have been uniformly successful because they were artistically gotten up, pleasing to the eye and ear and not tediously long."[4]

Later that year the Martinettis presented the best of several San Francisco versions of *The Black Crook*—a hugely popular dance-theater epic considered the mother of the Broadway musical and the show that legitimized the exposed-leg chorus line. Their staging was such a hit that they revived it in 1870, with the much-admired La Rita Sangalli imported for the lead. The *Bulletin's* review of Sangalli's performance reveals, typically, less about the dance than the dancer: "Her style . . . is unique. Indeed she may be said to have created a school of her own. Less arch and vivacious, and perhaps less airy in her movements than [Marie] Bonfanti [the original star of *The Black Crook*], she is more classical, more severely artistic, more surprisingly lithe of limb. Her poses are the perfection of grace. She executes the most difficult steps with an ease, freedom and abandon, at once pleasing and startling."[5]

The Black Crook was frequently revived in San Francisco and spawned a bevy of spin-offs. Increasingly elaborate and exotic, with plots based on historical incidents or well-known myths, these escapist musicals were in a sense the American equivalent of the English pantos. They even used some of the same story lines, embellishing them with catchier music, livelier action, more elaborate settings, and bigger, flashier everything.

Of the dozens of extravaganzas that played in San Francisco around this time, some of the most eye-popping and crowd-pleasing—*Antiope, Excelsior, Columbus and the Discovery of America,* tableau versions of Jules Verne's *A Trip to the Moon* and *Around the World in Eighty Days*— were the handiwork of the Kiralfy Brothers, a family of Hungarian choreographers who had a string of successes on Broadway. Other touring spectacles bore the stamp of David Henderson, the Chicago Opera House manager whose "Chicago-style" musicals poured on extra layers of glitz.

The Kiralfy Brothers' Excelsior *opened in New York in 1883 and arrived in San Francisco the following year, glorifying "the triumph of electric light over darkness." Until the 1880s, lighting for dance performances was provided solely by gas lamps, which contributed to an enormous number of fires and injuries. But with the advent of electric light and advances in theatrical machinery, new (and safer) forms of theatrical decoration came into vogue.*

At the Baldwin, the Grand Opera House, the California, and later the Columbia, these terpsichorean epics sold well. So did such displays of lavish exotica as *Sinbad, Aladdin, or The Wonderful Lamp, Bluebeard,* and, in quite another vein, *Africa!,* an extravagant and nonsensical show about an explorer, boasting a chorus of African American dancers.

The excess did not diminish with the new century. In 1904 the Columbia Theater presented *Around the World in Eighty Days* with an "Oriental ballet by fifty girls choreographed by Bothwell Browne," plus a heartily applauded "champagne dance and a Persian scarf dance."[6] That was topped in 1905 with a *Mother Goose* at the Grand Opera House that included a mind-boggling "L'Art Nouveau" ballet, featuring some four hundred performers who displayed "carved ivory, wrought bronzes and iron, mosaics, iridescent glasses, earthenware, limoges [china], enamels, gold work, transparent enamels, jewelry, and the diamond" as they moved.[7]

Dance segments were only one component of these spectacles, but they were often show-stoppers. Novelty routines (volcano, skirt, and scarf dances), richly costumed line processionals by huge choruses, and dizzying displays by featured ballerinas could be counted on to elicit cheers.

In 1889 the Great Kiralfy Ballet Troupe brought not one but two virtuoso *prima assolutas*, Mlle Paris and Mlle Carmencita, to appear in *Antiope* at the California Theater. An astute critic for the *Argonaut* analyzed both their styles. The big solo by the La Scala–trained Mlle Paris was described as a *"tour de force* that raises your wonder, but not your admiration. Looking at Mlle Paris flying across the stage on the tips of her toes, one cannot but marvel at the agility and dexterity of her movements, but of grace there is none. . . . She is more like a piece of steel mechanism than a woman, every movement exact, but there is no individuality."

Carmencita, on the other hand, was "all personality. . . . There is no observable method in her wild posturing, or perpetual sinuous motions, but there is something barbaric in their unrestrained spontaneity. Carmencita looks as if she might invent her strange dance as she went along, inspired by the rhythmic throb of the music."[8]

Most of the dancing San Francisco theatergoers saw in this period probably fell into one of these two camps: the steely mechanistic or the garishly undisciplined. But suddenly, just when America needed them, the rebels began to appear—independent-minded, homegrown movers, determined to free the dance from its prison of commerciality and frivolity, eager to explore its enormous potential as an expressive medium.

Not incidentally, most of these rebels were female, and their efforts to liberate the dance overlapped with the first surges of the women's suffrage movement. Nor is it surprising that several major dance innovators were Californians. Despite its growing reliance on imported entertainment, the youthful state was still wide open to experimentation in many fields. And the majesty of the natural environment, its neo-Mediterranean contours, climate, and ambience, inspired creative idealism in dancers as it had in painters, writers, and architects.

Isadora Duncan, a great American dance pioneer, was both a true daughter of Northern California and an original who invented herself *sui generis*. During her girlhood in San Francisco and Oakland, Isadora's passion for ancient Greek culture fused with her burning desire to create a dance as freely, boldly American as the roiling Pacific surf, the High Sierra, and the odes of Walt Whitman. To historian Kevin Starr, the youthful Duncan represented a "bold fulfillment of the Mediterranean metaphor that animated so much turn-of-the-century California creativity. In her search for something joyous and Greek, something healthy and beauteous,

The Spanish dancer Carmencita, a star in the Kiralfys' musical Antiope, *danced in an impassioned style that was the extreme opposite of the cool precision offered by many European prima ballerinas. One disgruntled San Francisco critic objected to her "wild posturing" and "perpetual sinuous motions," noting "something barbaric in their unrestrained spontaneity."*

the young Isadora Duncan, seeking her Grecian ideal, was seeking a California ideal as well."[9]

Much has been written about Duncan's triumphs as a performer, her impact on dancers of her own and succeeding generations, her flamboyant love affairs, and her agonizing personal tragedies. Less well known, but very pertinent to her development as an artist and a woman, were her formative years in the Bay Area. In middle age Isadora would express ambivalence about San Francisco, and as a teenager she couldn't leave the city fast enough. But she always acknowledged how much California had shaped her complex character.

Isadora's background was woven from two quintessentially San Franciscan strands: the hardy Gold Rush pioneer experience and the romance of West Coast bohemianism. Isadora's maternal grandparents, the Grays, were proud, ambitious Irish immigrants who came to California via covered wagon in 1850. Her upstanding grandfather, Thomas Gray, operated the first Oakland–San Francisco ferry service, served in the State Assembly, and was appointed to a high U.S. Naval post by President Andrew Johnson.

In contrast, Isadora's paternal side was dominated by the charismatic, elusive figure of her father, Joseph Charles Duncan. Duncan also arrived in San Francisco in 1850—but with a different agenda. An erudite Philadelphia transplant with a flair for art and commerce, Duncan worked in journalism, auctioneering, and finance while writing well-regarded poems and criticism, collecting art, and consorting with the *Golden Era* literary set. Much to Thomas Gray's chagrin, his sensitive and musically talented twenty-year-old daughter Mary Dora (called Dora) became the second wife of fifty-year-old Joseph Duncan. In short order they produced two daughters and two sons; Isadora, the youngest, was born May 26, 1877.[10] In her spottily reliable autobiography, *My Life*, Isadora recalled dancing in her mother's womb and being inspired by her father's collection of classical Greek sculptures. "While playing in the garden of my father's house," she wrote, "I tried by instinct to impart to my childish dance what I saw exhibited in the models of art."[11]

Actually, she was only a babe in arms when her father deserted the family. Two financial institutions run by Duncan collapsed in the wake of the silver crash, and a nasty scandal ensued. Unlike Billy Ralston, who wasn't around to face the music, Duncan was accused in the press of reckless speculation and "financial depravity" and was even jailed briefly

Although unable to accomplish all she set out to do, Isadora Duncan made a profound impact on her culture and her time. As dance historian Margaretta Mitchell has written, "A true California daughter, Duncan trusted her own nature, studied herself—saw her art and life as inextricably connected. . . . Her dance, like much California art of the time, echoed the rhythms of nature: she was a pure expression of the body in space, free from narrative, character, and plot, dance as spiritual imperative."

for embezzlement. The charge didn't stick but he fled the city in disgrace, leaving his wife and children to fend for themselves. "All my childhood," Isadora later noted, "seemed to be under the black shadow of this mysterious father of whom no one would speak."[12]

After this keening blow, Dora Duncan took her brood to Oakland and struggled to make ends meet by giving piano lessons, sewing, and moving whenever the landlord threatened eviction. It must have been a humiliating way of life, but Isadora later swore there were compensations. "Even though our mother couldn't give us enough physical food," she recalled, "she did give us enough spiritual food. When she played Schubert and Beethoven for us, or read to us from Shakespeare and Shelley and Browning, we forgot our hunger and cold."[13]

Apparently Dora was so preoccupied with eking out a living that she granted her children an unusual degree of independence, even allowing Isadora to drop out of public school at age ten. Isadora was later grateful to her mother for leaving her children "free to follow our own vagabond impulses. . . . To this wild untrammeled life of my childhood I owe the inspiration of the dance I created, which was but the expression of freedom."[14]

Although she had despised the rote drudgery of school, Isadora became an avid reader of the classics as well as a student of gymnastics, drama, and dance. She responded passionately to the exalted Golden Age of Greece depicted in Greek statuary, plays, and pottery, and reinvoked in romantic poems such as John Keats' "Ode on a Grecian Urn" and contemporary Bay Area architecture. These interests she shared with a good childhood friend, Florence Treadwell. (Decades later the married Florence Treadwell Boynton would leave her own mark on Bay Area dance by erecting the Temple of the Wings, a Grecian home and Duncan-style dance school in the Berkeley hills.) Some dance historians believe the young Isadora also studied the Delsarte method, a philosophy of voice, gesture, and body movement devised by the late French educator and theorist Francois Delsarte. Delsarte believed that what is natural is most beautiful and that all natural sounds and gestures are deeply expressive of spiritual and emotional states. The American teachings based on his ideas promoted the wearing of Grecian robes and the striking of classical poses.[15]

Nature and dance became Isadora's spiritual refuges. By her account, during her dreamy but determined adolescence she "often ran away alone into the woods or to the beach by the sea, and there I danced. I felt even then that my shoes and my clothes only hindered me. . . . So I took everything off. And without any eyes watching me, entirely alone, I danced, naked by the sea."[16]

Dance also helped keep the wolf from the Duncan door. Isadora's three older siblings earned money teaching social dances (polkas, waltzes), and eventually she joined them. In 1894 Isadora was advertising her own "Instruction in the Dance and Delsarte" in the San Francisco Directory. Even then, at seventeen, she was teaching in a style of classical simplicity

The Temple of the Wings in Berkeley, California, was another outgrowth of the Bay Area's love affair with the Hellenistic ideal. Conceived by Isadora Duncan's childhood friend Florence Treadwell Boynton—and designed in the first stages by the great architect Bernard Maybeck—the Temple was finally rendered by Randolph Monro and constructed in 1914. Boynton's heirs continue to live in this unusual house where generations of Bay Area children have learned dance in the Duncan style.

While still in her teens, Isadora Duncan appeared as a winged dancing fairy in an Augustin Daly production of A Midsummer Night's Dream, *which toured to cities around the country (including San Francisco) in 1896. Isadora's weekly salary was a welcome $15 (half of it sent home to her mother), but her work in the commercial theater proved very unsatisfying. "I was extremely unhappy," she recalled in her autobiography. "My dreams, my ideals, my ambition: all seemed futile. I made very few friends in the company. They regarded me as queer."*

that was antithetical to the theatrical garishness and balletic rigidity of the day, a simplicity as natural as the movement patterns of ocean waves. Intuitively, the young Isadora decided that dance must renew its contact with the earth, aim for the highest spiritual summit, and evolve from the simplest, most organic of physical movements—running, skipping, leaping, standing, reaching.

"We called it a new system of dancing, but in reality there was no system," Duncan wrote of her classes in *My Life*. "I followed my fantasy and improvised, teaching any pretty thing that came into my head. One of my first dances was Longfellow's poem, 'I shot an arrow into the air.' I used to recite the poem and teach the children to follow its meaning in gesture and movement."[17]

Decades later, poet Flora Jacobi Arnstein recalled taking Isadora's early classes. The students never improvised, she said, but performed precise gestures dictated by Duncan, "who was attired in a flowing white robe, tied by a gold cord under her bosom." Her teacher, Arnstein told Duncan biographer Millicent Dillon, was like "a spirit from another world."[18]

By that point Isadora had settled on her perfect dance costume: her "little white Greek tunic," similar to the attire favored by Delsarte's disciples. This draped, unrestricting garment was a kind of manifesto, a blatant rejection of the whalebone corsets, thick tights, stiff tutus, and tortuous toe-shoes most female dancers wore at the time. "When I dance, I use my body as a musician uses his instrument, as a painter uses his palette and brush, and as a poet uses the images of his mind," Duncan would later explain. "It has never dawned on me to swathe myself in hampering garments or to bind my limbs and drape my throat, for am I not striving to fuse soul and body in one unified image of beauty?"[19]

In about 1893, the absent Joseph Duncan resurfaced in San Francisco. He had amassed a new fortune (and begun a new family) in Los Angeles, and to atone for past sins he bestowed on Dora a large city house on Sutter and Van Ness streets. This made the next two years easier for Isadora and her siblings, and they stepped up their artistic pursuits. Brother Augustin turned the backyard barn into a theater and produced shows there: he recited poetry, Isadora danced, brother Raymond and sister Elizabeth also performed. They even took their family show on the road, visiting Santa Clara, Santa Barbara, and Santa Rosa. Archivist Russell Hartley has tracked down a charming portrait of the dewy Isadora in this period, credited to a

Fresno photographer. Clad in a soft white dress, she cradles a wreath as though it were a magic talisman of ancient Greece.

San Francisco helped mold Isadora's genius but could not contain it—just as it could nurture but not meet the grand ambitions of David Belasco, Lotta Crabtree, and so many other rising young artists. The immediate catalyst for Duncan's departure was financial necessity: her father went bust yet again, and the comfortable home he had given Dora was lost. Although aflame with the aspirations of an artistic revolutionary, eighteen-year-old Isadora was pragmatic enough to think she could best support her family by working in the commercial theater. In June 1895 she left with her mother for Chicago, where dance jobs were more plentiful.

But Isadora left for other reasons too. The nonconforming child of a scandalous father, she ran up against the puritanical side of San Francisco, a side that less extreme rebels never encountered. "The dominant note of my childhood was the constant spirit of revolt against the narrowness of the society in which we lived, against the limitations of life and a growing desire to fly eastward to something I imagined might be broader," she said in her autobiography. "How often I remembered haranguing the family and my relations, and always ending with, 'We *must* leave this place, we shall never be able to accomplish anything here.' "[20]

Duncan was probably too unconventional in thought and deed for any American city of her era. In Chicago she lasted only a short time as a dancer with Augustin Daly's popular theater troupe. (She stayed long enough to return to San Francisco with them in May 1896, as a reluctant fairy in *A Midsummer Night's Dream*.) Moving on to New York, Isadora did perform solo dances—but won favor only in the parlors of society women. Manhattanites reacted to her bare feet, Greek costume, simple gestures, classical piano accompaniments, and outspoken feminism with either faddish glee or jocular scorn.

Leaving behind the New World, Isadora turned to the more hospitable shores of Europe. After sailing with her family to London in 1899, she visited her beloved Greece (and fantasized setting up a school there), played to large, rapturous audiences in Paris, triumphed in Germany.

As Duncan's fame grew, San Francisco newspapers began claiming her as a native daughter, tracking her exploits. But mingled with the pride in her achievements was the skepticism that Isadora would always encounter in America. A 1903 story in the *Call* reported that her German performances

Isadora Duncan appears here with Patrick, one of her two adored children, around 1910. The greatest tragedy of her life (from which she never truly recovered) was the loss of Patrick and her daughter, Deirdre, in a 1913 drowning accident in Paris. Responding to the outpouring of condolences from friends and strangers, Isadora sent the following note to the press: "My friends have helped me to realize what alone could comfort me. That all men are my brothers, all women are my sisters and all little children on earth are my children." But when she visited San Francisco four years later, in 1917, Isadora's grief was still palpable.

commanded ticket prices "as high as those of Coquelin and Mme [Sarah] Bernhardt." But the paper couldn't resist reminding readers that Isadora's father was a "notorious embezzler," and it invited Lola Yberri, a far from objective rival dancer, to assess her art. "Miss Duncan doesn't dance at all," Lola hissed, "she just poses. She made a dismal failure when she appeared as a star in New York City."[21]

An *Examiner* article of the same vintage also mentioned Isadora's scoundrel father, but offered more credible dance analysis: "It is not the rapidly whirling skirts of the fandango or the sand-scattering buck-and-wing dance, or in anything else modern to which the ballerina pirouettes across the stage, that Miss Duncan has made her great hit. . . . Nothing less than Greek dances, Roman posturings and the most classic of gyrations satisfy the endeavors of Miss Duncan."[22]

By 1910 the *Examiner* was calling Duncan "the American high priestess of the classic style of dancing."[23] Although her adopted daughters, the Isadorables, performed in San Francisco, Isadora revisited the city only once, in November 1917. She was then nearly forty and one of the world's most famous (and controversial) women. The fates had been both cruel and kind to her. She was now an acclaimed and influential artist, but the death of her two small children and her failure to establish a permanent school weighed heavily on her soul.

San Francisco welcomed her back for two weeks of concerts at the Columbia Theater with a fanfare of publicity. The ads announced that she would perform some of her most famous dances—to *La Marseillaise*, Gluck's *Iphigenia in Aulis*, and Tchaikovsky's *Pathétique* Symphony— among other works played live by a sixty-member orchestra and famed pianist Harold Bauer.

Socialites more familiar with Isadora's brazen love affairs than her dance philosophy snapped up the seats to her November 25 opening. And though the soul-scarred, hard-living Isadora was no longer a radiant slip of a girl, her performance that day and in her subsequent local concerts won over the skeptics. Even Josephine Hart Phelps, a wary *Argonaut* reviewer, admitted, "I do not say she herself is beautiful, she is so neither in face nor in figure, but her art is exquisite, and can, in flashes, transform."[24]

Far less restrained was the *Examiner*'s Redfern Mason. Mason interviewed Duncan at length in her hotel room and lauded her in reviews. He got so cozy with the dancer that he even let her pen, under his own

This portrait captures a very young Isadora, posing in an Oakland photography studio. Around this time she was living with her mother and siblings in the East Bay, in much-reduced circumstances after the sudden departure of her disgraced financial speculator father, Joseph Duncan. It would be many years before Isadora reestablished contact with her father, whom she described later as a "black shadow" hovering over her childhood.

byline, a glowing report of a solo piano concert played by Harold Bauer in her benefit. In his review of Isadora's first concert Mason gushed, "The dance is of the spirit as well as of the flesh, and it is because she has a great soul that Isadora Duncan outpeers all her sisters." Of her Iphigenia he wrote, "Here is no slavish copying of the poses of the nymphs on the Parthenon, but rather the functioning of the spirit which inspired the hand of Phidias and Praxiteles, lent ecstasy to the verse of Sappho and caused the genius of Pindar to burn with lava heat." Mason's own mission was stated in his closing: "Miss Duncan has come back to her own people and they pay her the tribute which is due to inspired art."[25]

Isadora probably had the most impact, however, on the budding dancers in her audiences. Lenore Peters Job, who later ran a major dance studio in San Francisco, recalled her own reaction to Duncan in "the famous *Marseillaise*." Said Job, "In her passionate fervor she rent her garments, revealing her bare breasts to public view. In a day when her appearance in bare feet and filmy chiffon was something of a shock, this was a daring feat. As I watched spellbound, I felt that I was seeing the human spirit released from bondage."[26]

Duncan's San Francisco homecoming was an artistic success, but bittersweet personally. Rumor had it that the dancer was carrying on an imprudent affair with the married Harold Bauer. Because of a previous problem with her brother Raymond, the University of California trustees had withheld permission for Duncan to perform in the Greek Theater. Adding injury to insult, Isadora's drunken manager ran off with some of the money from her successful Columbia Theater run, while much of the rest of it was squandered on parasitic hangers-on who drank and ate at her expense. (Harold Bauer saved the day with that benefit concert.)

At the time, Florence Boynton and others were planning to build a Duncan school in the Bay Area, but financial obstacles caused delays. Isadora, who left the city abruptly, later recounted her frustration with the visit: "I was despondent at the lack of response of my native town to support my ideal of a future School. They had a crowd of my imitators and several imitation schools already, with which they seemed quite satisfied, and they even seemed to think that the sterner stuff of my Art might cause some disaster. My imitators had become all saccharine and sweet syrup, promulgating that part of my work which they were pleased to call the 'harmonious and beautiful!' but omitting anything sterner, omitting,

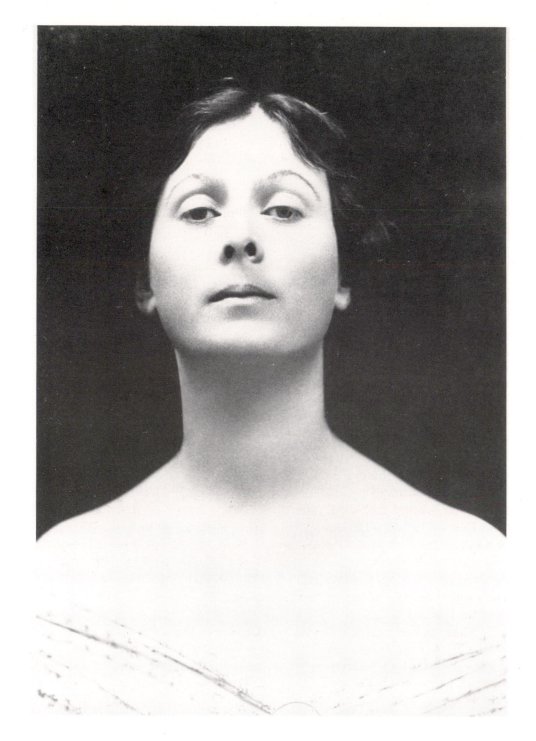

Arnold Genthe, the famed photographer best known for his images of San Francisco's Chinatown, immortalized Isadora Duncan's tranquil, long-stemmed beauty in this classic portrait. Genthe was a confidante and great admirer of the dancer and took many memorable photographs of her in repose and in action. The best were collected in his photo anthology, The Book of the Dance. *In another book,* On with the Dance, *Genthe wrote of Isadora,* "Her endowment is no mere talent for the consummation of exterior beauties; it is genius. She is a seer and a prophet, fulfilled of understanding and wisdom."

in fact, the mainspring and real meaning."[27]

From Boynton's perspective, Duncan's departure was "a great disappointment to the general public and especially to those who had waited years for her coming, to establish her school; but we all believed she would some day in the near future return in full glory to triumphantly fulfill all her hopes and ours."[28] But Duncan never returned to San Francisco. Eight years later she was killed in a freak auto accident.

Although she did not realize all her own dreams, Isadora, in Agnes de Mille's view, "touched off a creative conflagration. . . . She preached a return to classic simplicity and pagan joy at the precise moment in history when our civilization was moving forward into a new era, when freedoms of all kinds were being sought—economic, political, social and spiritual."[29]

While Duncan is by far the best known dance innovator of her era, there were other American women conducting their own movement experiments around the same time. One was Illinois native Loie Fuller, a visionary dancer whose spectacular use of colored lighting and voluminous, abstract costumes delighted San Francisco during her first performances in the city in 1896. A minor but intriguing figure was the Northern California–bred Maud Allan, creator of the famous *Vision of Salome* dance.

Born Maud Allan Durrant in Toronto, Canada, in 1873, Allan grew up in San Francisco and studied music locally at Cogswell's College. In 1895 her ambitious mother, who was convinced that the lithe and pretty Maud had a future as a concert pianist, contrived to send her to Germany for further training at the Berlin Royal Academy.

During her long stay in Europe, Maud branched out beyond music to study painting and sculpture in Italy. She had less formal dance training than Duncan but, like her, found much inspiration in art and music— particularly the visual masterworks of Ancient Greece and the Renaissance, and music by European classical composers. (Also like Isadora, Allan was haunted by a scandal involving a close male relative. Her beloved brother Theo was convicted of killing two women and was executed in 1897 at San Quentin Prison.)

Allan, in her memoirs, traced her first dance impulses to a viewing of Botticelli's famous *Primavera:* "As I stood before [it], entranced by the rhythm and the flowing lines of the dancing graces, all my indefinite longings and vague inspirations crystallized into a distinct idea. Art is a

Loie Fuller created a sensation when she performed at the California Theater in 1896. An innovator whose work presaged that of later choreographers such as Alwin Nikolais, Fuller combined lighting effects with abstract costuming and coordinated movement to magical effect. Although she was not the first to project colored lights onto silk cloth, Fuller was the most artistically successful. Her precisely designed solo dances took the form of swirling, phantasmagorical works, or of luminescent kinetic sculptures. In Lily of the Nile, *for example, she carefully draped her body in five hundred yards of billowing white silk and, according to a* San Francisco Chronicle *review, "waved slowly . . . [until] those rolls of silk wound upward into the enormous and perfect flower standing at its highest tip fifteen feet above the stage—the white calla of the Nile." Fuller formed a special bond with San Francisco and returned later to choreograph the opening dance procession for the 1915 Panama Pacific International Exposition. She also encouraged her friend Alma Spreckels, a San Francisco philanthropist, to acquire a collection of Rodin sculptures for the city's new art museum, the Palace of the Legion of Honor.*

CALIFORNIA THEATRE

AL. HAYMAN CO. (INCORPORATED), Proprietors

LA LOIE FULLER

method of expression, the expression of feelings and thoughts through beautiful movements, shapes and sounds. To try to express in movement the emotions and thoughts stirred by melody, beautiful pictures and sculpture had become my ambition."[30]

Making the most of her limited gifts, Allan would forge an "aesthetic" dance career that corresponded both to the classicism of Duncan and to the decadent side of *fin de siècle* art championed by contemporaries like Oscar Wilde (who also made use of the Salome tale). Her emotive, seemingly spontaneous dances, some of which borrowed themes from literature and art, were undulant "visualizations" of works by Bach, Beethoven, Chopin, Schubert, and other well-known composers. She made her concert debut in Vienna, Austria, in 1903, opening with an impressionistic dance to Mendelssohn's *Spring Song*. In 1904 she was invited to the Bayreuth Festival to "interpret" the operas of Richard Wagner. Sporadic appearances around Europe followed.

Allan's period of blazing celebrity began in 1908, with the London premiere of *The Vision of Salome* at the Palace Theater. Allan was not the only one to turn the biblical Salome story into a dance; veil-swishing numbers enjoyed quite a vogue early in the century. Her imaginative rendition (influenced by the famous Max Reinhardt production of Wilde's *Salome*) was a stand-out, however, and apparently the most provocative number in her repertoire. In it, Allan displayed a highly suggestive stage demeanor, a loftiness of aesthetic purpose, plus the courage to dance barefoot (still very unusual at the time), sway and weave sensuously in revealing garb, and fondle the decapitated (mock) head of Saint John the Baptist.

According to biographer Felix Cherniavsky, Allan "presented Salome as a *femme fatale* and as decadence incarnate"—certainly a post-Victorian interpretation, and a brave exhibition of female sexuality for the time. Though some English clergy mounted protests, the British press reacted orgasmically to the dance and praised it in the most breathless terms. The London *Observor* critic wrote of Maud, "Her writhing body enacts the whole voluptuousness of Eastern femininity."[31] That was topped by the *Labour Leader*: "Her slender and lissom body writhes in an ecstasy of fear, quivers at the exquisite touch of pain, laughs and sighs, shrinks and vaults, as swayed by passion. One moment her dancing is hot, barbaric, lawless; the next, grotesque, sinister, repulsive. . . . London has never seen such graceful and artistic dancing. It is of a magical beauty."[32]

Today the "Salome" sounds like sexy kitsch, but then it was sensational and unusual enough to catapault Allan to international fame. She performed on several continents, and at thirty-five wrote her autobiography, *My Life and Dancing*. In 1910 she played in San Francisco during a tour of the United States, performing at the Garrick Theater with a forty-five-piece symphony orchestra. Though San Francisco audiences cheered her appearance, local reviewers of Allan's April 5, 1910, opening did not register unanimous admiration. In his *Chronicle* notice, Ralph E. Renaud gave the majority view: "To all who seek the true soul of music, and to all who are awake to the romance and emotion which lie just below the surface of everyday life, last night at the Garrick Theater was a night . . . to be remembered, treasured, and . . . reverenced."[33]

Of another mind was George L. Shoals, an *Argonaut* critic. He lumped Allan together with Hawaiian hula dancers and grumbled, "To call her work intrepretation of music, music that was written without thought of the dance . . . is as far removed from sound judgement as the ecstasy of lingering looks on languid lilies so earnestly aspired to by the Wilde followers." He went on to twist the knife: "It is not believable that the rising generation will be taught to find the only true expression of one of Mendelssohn's 'songs without words' in the amblings and writhings of a barefoot girl on a green-curtained stage."[34]

Allan's star began to fade soon after that American tour. The fad for aesthetic dancing was on the wane, and the Salome vogue had been exhausted. An egocentric, domineering person who could be her own worst enemy, Allan kept touring for the next decade. But new modern dance forms were emerging, and Allan couldn't or wouldn't adapt to them. By 1925 her stardom was over. Financially strapped from then on, she lived into her eighties, her performing career an obscure footnote in dance history until her recent rediscovery by feminist scholars.

Neither Duncan, Allan, nor Fuller created a specific dance technique for dancers of the future to build on. That was left to other bold movers of the early twentieth century, including such Californians as Ruth St. Denis, Ted Shawn, and Martha Graham. But modern dance's earliest pioneers still deserve much credit for their break-through contributions. It took the unorthodox "amblings and writhings," not to mention the emancipated attitudes, of barefoot California girls like Isadora Duncan and Maud Allan to set America's art-dance movement in motion.

Maud Allan strikes poses from one of her best-known works, a dance to Felix Mendelssohn's Spring Song. Bred in San Francisco, the beautiful young Allan turned to dance after studying music in Berlin. Like Isadora Duncan, she performed in bare feet, sometimes in ancient Greek costume, and often to well-known works of classical music. But Allan insisted that she was not an imitator of Duncan's, and her "aesthetic dancing" career (which began in 1903) followed a very different course. Indeed, her greatest triumph occurred in a piece that would be unimaginable for Isadora: a sexually suggestive turn as the biblical bad girl Salome, in which she writhed around the stage brandishing the decapitated head of Saint John the Baptist.

Earthquake Eve on the Town:
April 17, 1906

April 17, 1906, was a Tuesday, and at the time San Francisco's Tuesday nights were lively. If you were inclined to spend the evening out and about (and many were), an assortment of dramatic and musical possibilities awaited. As befit the era, most of the city's theaters had scheduled diverting amusements, with little about them to tax the intellect or trouble the soul. That still left plenty of room for the variety (and wide range of quality) that San Franciscans had grown accustomed to in their cultural bazaar.

Grand opera and light operetta, vaudeville and variety, farce and burlesque, and (of course) melodrama were all advertised on local marquees that evening, at prices ranging from ten cents (for vaudeville) to seven dollars (for the best seat at the opera). No one could have known that the very next night the lights of every theater in town would be extinguished and the world's attention would be riveted on a San Francisco saga far more awe-inspiring than any sensation-melodrama.

The stage setting for this epic? A fast-paced, still-growing city, the nation's sixth largest metropolis with a population (as of the 1900 census) of over 342,782 people. No longer dependent on gold and silver strikes, San Francisco was enjoying a more stable form of prosperity. It had become the financial center for California's bullish agricultural business and the site of more foreign and domestic trade than any American city outside New York.

The town was proud of its up-to-dateness, glorying in technological developments that affected the theater along with other spheres. A new ferry made it easier for Oakland residents to travel across the Bay to catch shows. Electric beams had replaced gas footlights. Cable cars and motorized vehicles crowded the horsedrawn carriages at the curbsides of theaters.

San Francisco still had its boundless *joie de vivre*, its reputation for being the most happy-go-lucky and charismatic of American cities: hence such tributes as prizefighter Jimmie Britt's famous remark, "I'd rather be a busted lamp post on Battery Street . . . than the Waldorf-Astoria."[1] But despite its chronically effervescent spirits, the community had been confronting some serious urban problems. A gruesome epidemic of bubonic plague had lasted four years in San Francisco; it finally ended in 1904,

"They all retired, the good and the bad, unconscious of the danger. So far as the records show no one indulged in the familiar if unwarranted meteorological assumption that it seemed like earthquake weather. . . . Those who had sought their pillows humming refrains from Carmen *and the others who wooed sleep at an earlier hour from the late revelers, were alike oblivious of the rude awakening that awaited them early in the morning."*

John Young
San Francisco: A History of the Pacific Coast Metropolis
1912

*"Put me somewhere west of East Street
   where there's nothin' left but dust,
Where the lads are all a bustlin' and
   where everything's gone bust,
Where the buildin's that are standin'
   sort of blink and blindly stare
At the damndest finest ruins ever
   gazed on anywhere."*

Larry Harris
"The Damndest Finest Ruins"
1906

133

AFTER THE QUAKE: SARAH BERNHARDT AT THE GREEK THEATER, MAY 17, 1906

after an all-out war on rats. Alcoholism was rampant, as were prostitution and sexual diseases in the more unsavory areas of town. Crippling mass strikes in 1901 by disgruntled workers presaged more labor strife on the horizon. (Around this time a national unionization movement among actors was also picking up steam.) Unregulated development had made the architectural landscape a hodgepodge of prim Victorian homes, pretentious stone buildings (like the expensive boondoggle of a city hall), and slapdash older wooden structures. Chinatown, though a picturesque tourist attraction, was also a cramped, dingy ghetto.

Mayor Eugene "Handsome Gene" Schmitz embodied the city's dual personality. When first elected in 1901, Schmitz was the musical director at the Columbia Theater and president of the local Musicians' Union. His showmanship, good looks, and German-Irish ancestry helped him at the ballot box, and he won reelection twice. By 1906, however, both press and public knew the maestro was merely the puppet of corrupt Abe Ruef, a shrewd backroom boss who ruled the city by graft and patronage and who did little to remedy its urban ills.

The Ruef-Schmitz scandal was big news, but on the night of April 17, 1906, San Francisco's social and political nobility had something else on its mind: opera. Leading singers from New York's Metropolitan Opera Company had arrived at the Grand Opera House for a two-week season under the direction of Heinrich Conried. On April 16 the troupe opened with Karl Goldmark's *The Queen of Sheba*. The social set thronged to this biblical epic, which was apparently most notable for a $40,000 set depicting King Solomon's garden and temple. (In the April 17 *Examiner*, music critic Ashton Stevens complained, "Some sort of a shock is supposed to go with a seven-dollar seat, but last night never touched us." Another kind of shock would come soon enough.)

Many opera lovers returned on April 17 for the Met's much-anticipated production of *Carmen* by Georges Bizet. Mezzo-soprano Olive Fremstad sang the title role, Bessie Abott performed Micaela, and Arturo Vigna conducted. But the star was undeniably the thrilling young Italian tenor Enrico Caruso, who had performed in the city once before and was making a triumphant return as Don Jose. (Upon his arrival, reported the *Call*, Caruso's "delight at being back in San Francisco again was manifested in a choice assortment of Italian adjectives.")[2]

For *Carmen*, the Opera House's boxes were filled with grande dames

Fabled tenor Enrico Caruso entranced the city's opera lovers with his charismatic Don Jose in Carmen *the night before the Great Earthquake struck. The next morning, deeply shaken by the calamity (in more ways than one), Caruso reportedly ran out of his hotel room into the quake-damaged streets clutching an autographed portrait of President Theodore Roosevelt. He tried out his voice to see if it still worked and promptly grabbed the first boat to Oakland. Caruso swore he would never return to San Francisco, and throughout his glorious career he never did.*

like Mrs. Charles de Young (wife of the *Chronicle*'s publisher) and Mrs. James Flood (wife of the railroad baron). Madame Flood came close to blinding people with her diamond tiara, diamond "dog-collar" necklace, and gown with a diamond front and diamond shoulder straps.[3] A less flashy audience member was twenty-four-year-old John Barrymore, Jr., a scion of the great Barrymore acting clan.[4]

But the evening belonged to Caruso. According to Blanche Partington's rapturous notice for the early morning *Chronicle* of April 18 (an edition few would read), "The audience forgot its diamonds. . . . [It] forgot everything but the electric performance of Caruso, the wonderful." The "intelligent" Miss Fremstad contributed a "flash or two," but it was "Caruso the magician" who set off fireworks. Partington praised not just the tenor's voice, but his comic byplay and the "simply sizzling" excitement he generated in his final scene: "Lean of cheek, grief and madness staring from the eyes—pshaw! He made one forget that it was only an opera."

While some San Franciscans swooned over Caruso, others were lapping up the sugary sweetness of *Babes in Toyland*. Victor Herbert's comic operetta about enchanted playthings was in its second night at the Columbia Theater. The lavish production boasted a hundred-member cast, including Ignacio Martinetti of the Martinetti dance clan. The *Call* critic enthused, "*Babes in Toyland,* while not infantile, furnishes enough variety to be pleasing to a juvenile audience, while the older auditors see much to applaud and to laugh over."[5] Other operetta fans trekked to the Tivoli where *Miss Timidity* was playing—a sentimental musical that boasted the popular song "Mother, Mother, Mother, Pin a Rose on Me."[6]

Those in the mood for farce found it at the Alcazar Theater, where the stock players were romping through Leo Ditrichstein's *Are You a Mason?*, a mistaken-identity comedy with Charles Waldron and Ernest Glendenning in lead roles. The Majestic (a new theater that opened in 1904 with Mayor Schmitz's proclamation, "Majestic in name, let us hope it will ever stand for what is majestic in art!") hosted another farce, *Who Goes There?* The play starred and was written by local showman Walter Perkins, and Tuesday's performance was a benefit for Spanish American War veterans.[7]

The Orpheum and the Chutes sated the city's cravings for vaudeville. The Orpheum revue, trendily titled *Motoring*, featured "Charles R. Sweet; Armstrong and Holly; Mlle Lotty; The Famous Agoust Family; Goleman's Dogs, Cats and Doves; Jimmy Wall; Artie Hall and Orpheum Motion

The original Orpheum Theater lay in ruins after the April 1906 earthquake and fire. Virtually every playhouse in the city, with the exception of the Chutes and the South San Francisco Opera House, was destroyed in the disaster.

Pictures."[8] Out in the Avenues at the Chutes, local ballet instructor Mr. Bothwell Browne and his dancing Gaiety Girls presented the parodistic *Mikado on the Half Shell*. Comedian Ted E. Box, the Imperial Russian Dancers, and the animatoscope ("the latest novelties in moving pictures") filled out the bill, but theater patrons could also check out the Chutes' exhibit of rare animals or take a ride in its Touring Scenic Car.[9]

At the six-year-old Central Theater, run by Alcazar managers Fred C. Belasco and Milton Meyer, melodrama ruled. The April 17 offering was a typical weepie: *Dangers of the Working Girls*, starring Edna A. Crawford. Meanwhile, the Alhambra brought Theodore Kremer's melodrama *The Queen of the Highbinders* to a somewhat rougher crowd. A riot erupted in the balcony that night when a security guard tried to eject a catcaller from his seat and others loudly prevented him from doing so. "The whole house rose in an uproar," reported the *Call*. But "cooler heads prevailed and after the arrest of the ringleaders of the mob quiet was restored."[10]

The California Theater advertised "positively the best" in burlesque, with the Cherry Blossom Burlesquers in "Two Side-Splitting Burlettas: *The Wrong Count Tobacco* and *Quarrelsome Neighbors*." And though the newspapers don't mention it, there was probably a Chinese opera at Dan Sang Fung (also known as the Royal Chinese Theater) on Jackson Street and plenty of action in San Francisco's dance halls, honky-tonks, and cabarets.

After all the bows were taken and all the applause had died away, after all the *après*-theater parties ended and most of the city was fast asleep, the ground began to rumble. It was fourteen minutes past five in the morning when the first earthquake hit. In quick succession came another, then a devastating third. Walls tumbled. Buildings rocked off their foundations. Gas and water mains burst. Fires erupted, blanketing the city in thick black smoke and raging out of control for four days. By the time it was over, much of San Francisco lay in ruins.

"Not in history has a modern imperial city been so completely destroyed," wrote eyewitness Jack London, then an *Argonaut* reporter. "San Francisco is gone. Nothing remains of it but memories and a fringe of dwelling-houses on its outskirts. . . . All the shrewd contrivances and safeguards of man had been thrown out of gear by thirty seconds' twitching of the earth-crust."[11]

In the postquake panic, tens of thousands of people fled the flames. Among them was the previous night's toast of the town, Enrico Caruso. Legend has it that after being thrown out of bed by the seismic jolt, the tenor raced out of the Palace Hotel in his pajamas clutching an autographed portrait of President Theodore Roosevelt, tried out his voice to make sure it still worked, and caught one of the first boats to Oakland. One can only imagine what choice Italian adjectives he used to describe San Francisco on this occasion. In any case, he swore he would never return to the city, a promise he kept.

John Barrymore reacted to the cataclysm with less emotion—or so he later claimed. By his own account, the jaunty young actor wandered around Union Square in a tuxedo after the quake struck—first running into the distraught Caruso, later encountering the New York sport Diamond Jim Brady. While panic and chaos swirled around him, Barrymore supposedly returned to his room at the St. Francis Hotel and slept until late afternoon, when the encroaching fire finally drove him to seek refuge at a friend's home in Burlingame.[12]

Whatever the reactions of individual showpeople, one thing was clear: San Francisco had been largely reduced to ash and rubble, and 250,000 of its citizens were homeless. The city's theaters went the way of most other large buildings. All but one of the major houses perished in flames. Only the Chutes survived because, located in the Avenues, it was out of the path of the worst fires.

The luxurious 1903 Tivoli Opera House, built after the existing 1879 structure was declared a firetrap, was one of the many venues gutted by the post-earthquake blaze. Theatrical producers swiftly erected new theaters to replace those lost. The Tivoli (above) was eventually rebuilt and opened with great fanfare in 1913. But within a year the vogue for the motion picture had encroached on the market for family-style live musical theater, and the Tivoli was revamped into a cinema. The Davis Theater (below), one of the first new playhouses, was a good example of the slapdash temporary structures put up to replace the elegant old ones.

It is impossible not to see the 1906 earthquake and fire as a demarcation line in San Francisco history. At the time of the disaster, the city was already on the verge of a major social, political, and cultural shake-up. The old San Francisco, that freewheeling boomtown and magnet for reckless adventurers, had already faded into legend. Its fabled "golden age"—as a center of great drama, as a mythic frontier community and American Athens—existed now only in the roseate memories of oldtimers. A sprawling twentieth-century metropolis called the San Francisco Bay Area was springing up in its place.

As stunned as they were by the disaster that had befallen them, San Franciscans wasted little time grieving for what was lost. Marshaling help from many quarters, they rebuilt their city—and they did so in very short order, given the extent of the damage.

The entertainment scene also bounced back with remarkable gusto. The first postquake performance was a free concert at the Golden Gate Park bandshell on April 29, less than two weeks after the debacle. A thousand people, many of them camped out in the park after losing their homes, turned up to hear an open-air concert by a military band.

Theatrical producers sensed an immediate market for escapism and dreamed up ways to provide it. The management of the gutted Orpheum wasted no time in taking over the lease of the Chutes. It reopened on May 26 as the New Orpheum, with Valerie Bergere and Company topping the bill. A couple of minor Oakland theaters, the melodrama-oriented Ye Old Liberty Playhouse and the Macdonough Theater (a vaudeville house), stepped up operations and found new patrons among the many urban "refugees" temporarily living in the East Bay.

Thanks to lax building codes and another round of astonishing optimism, San Francisco was soon erecting almost as many theaters as it had lost. On June 4, young Sid Grauman (future proprietor of Grauman's Chinese Theater in Los Angeles) opened the New National Theater on Post and Steiner streets to replace his defunct Unique Theater, a variety hall. (The National's seats were pews salvaged from a ruined church.) On June 30, 1906, the makeshift Park Theater opened at Market and Eighth streets with a canvas roof and seating for seventeen hundred. *Hearts of Tennessee* by California writer Ulric Collins was the first attraction, starring a cast made up of "survivors" from the Alcazar and Majestic stock companies. (There appears to have been little loss of life in the theater community.)

More competition arrived that same night, when the Davis Theater on McAllister and Fillmore streets was inaugurated with a musical comedy. Within a year one could also patronize the Colonial Theater, the Novelty Theater, the American, the Van Ness, and new versions of the Alcazar and the Orpheum. Significantly, many of these hastily built playhouses (and others to follow) were designed for live performance *and* the screening of that exciting new amusement, the motion picture.

One of the more poignant displays of San Francisco's cultural endurance took place on May 17, 1906. The site was the Greek Theater, the open-air arena that symbolized Northern California's affinity for the sensibilities and ideals of ancient Greece. The star of the evening was Madame Sarah Bernhardt, an old and loyal friend of San Francisco.

Bernhardt had been visiting the United States when the earthquake struck, and she rushed to Chicago to participate in a benefit for its victims. Soon after, the great leading lady embarked on a tour of the West, often appearing with her company in a specially-outfitted tent.

Bernhardt's performance at the Greek Theater on that May afternoon was a heartfelt and generous gift to the city. Five thousand quake-weary people tramped up to the sylvan Berkeley hills to see the free show. It was a sunny, windswept day, and, in that magnificent arena surrounded by wooded hills and breathtaking vistas, the Divine Sarah reprised one of her triumphs: the titular role in Jean Racine's tragic *Phèdre*. Nearly sixty years old, she was still capable of stirring audiences to the marrow in the role of the doomed Greek queen.

To *Examiner* critic Ashton Stevens, Bernhardt seemed particularly "inspired" on this occasion. Her love-offering of *Phèdre* was "immortal," moving many in the audience to tears. Bernhardt herself later declared she "had never had such inspiration. In all my life there is no other day to match it."[13]

An aging nineteenth-century European acting goddess emoting on the sun-washed stage of the Greek Theater, captivating San Franciscans only a month after their city had been virtually destroyed—this image perfectly conveys the close of the romantic phase of San Francisco's stage history. It leaves the impression of a community at the end of one epoch and on the brink of a profoundly different one, a city ready for the brave new world of the future yet not quite willing (it would never be entirely willing) to relinquish the seductive mythology of its past.

THE DIVINE SARAH IN RACINE'S *PHEDRE*

Key:
1 – Colonial
2 – Belvedere
3 – Majestic
4 – Mission
5 – California
6 – unidentified
7 – Oberon
8 – La Bohème
9 – Columbia
10 – Grand Opera House
11 – Fischer's
12 – Alhambra
13 – Alcazar
14 – Tivoli
15 – Empire
16 – Broadway
17 – Hammond
18 – Orpheum
19 – unidentified
20 – Chutes (intact)
21 – Central
22 – Novelty
23 – Unique

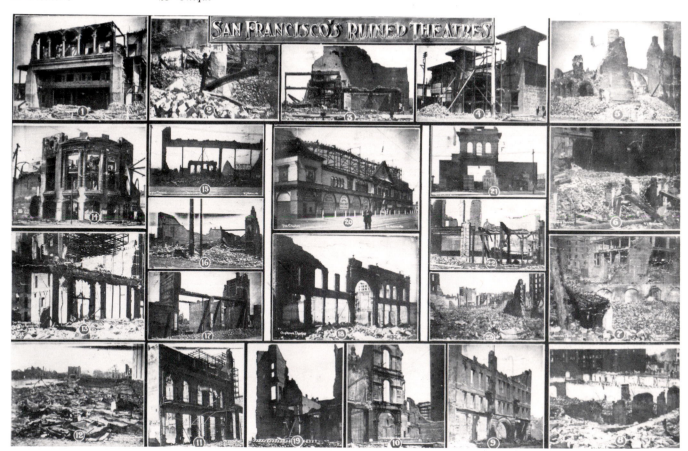

SAN FRANCISCO'S RUINED THEATRES

Photography Credits

All the images in this volume are drawn from the collection of the San Francisco Performing Arts Library & Museum (SF PALM), except for the photographs on pages 12, 14, and 103, which are included courtesy of the California Historical Society. We also acknowledge the Gabriel Moulin Studios for the Bohemian Grove images on pages 100, 104, and 105, and Margaretta K. Mitchell for her photograph of the Temple of the Wings on page 119. All posters are from the James H. Schwabacher Collection.

Notes

SAN FRANCISCO STAGE

[1] United States Census figures, quoted in Gladys Hansen, *The San Francisco Almanac* (San Rafael, Calif.: Presidio Press, 1980), 2.

[2] W. H. Bishop, "San Francisco," *Harper's New Monthly Magazine* 66 (May 1883): 313–32.

[3] Scott McElhaney, "The Professional Theatre in San Francisco, 1880–1889" (Ph.D. diss., Stanford University, 1972), 10.

[4] Excerpted in Oscar Lewis, *This Was San Francisco: Being First Hand Accounts of the Evolution of One of America's Favorite Cities* (New York: David McKay, 1962), 190.

[5] Ibid., 234.

THE SILVER ERA

[1] Lois Rather, *Bonanza Theatre* (Oakland, Calif.: Rather Press, 1977), 22.

[2] Ibid., 25.

[3] Walter Leman, *Memories of an Old Actor* (San Francisco: A. Roman & Co., 1886), 360.

[4] Mary Henderson, *Theatre in America* (New York: Harry N. Abrams, 1986), 143.

[5] Lawrence Estevan, ed., *San Francisco Theatre Research . . . Monographs* (San Francisco: Works Progress Administration, 1938–1942), 16:64.

[6] *San Francisco News Letter,* February 18, 1870.

[7] *San Francisco News Letter,* January 1, 1870.

[8] *San Francisco News Letter,* January 11, 1872.

[9] Oscar Lewis and Caroll D. Hall, *Bonanza Inn,* 2d ed. (New York: Ballantine Books, 1970), 11–18.

[10] *San Francisco News Letter,* August 28, 1875.

[11] *San Francisco Call,* August 27, 1875.

[12] Edmond M. Gagey, *The San Francisco Stage: A History* (New York: Columbia University Press, 1950), 130.

[13] *San Francisco Theatre Research* 16:222.

[14] Amelia Ransome Neville, *The Fantastic City: Memoirs of the Social and Romantic Life of Old San Francisco* (Boston: Houghton Mifflin, 1932), 266.

[15] Frederick Ross, *The Actor From Pt. Arena: Memories of an Old Theatrical Man* (Berkeley, Calif.: Friends of the Bancroft Library, University of California, 1977), 29.

[16] *San Francisco Chronicle,* July 22, 1877.

[17] Walter Krumm, "The San Francisco Stage, 1869–1879" (Ph.D. diss., Stanford University, 1959), 6.

DAVID BELASCO

[1] Craig Timberlake, *The Bishop of Broadway: The Life and Work of David Belasco* (New York: Library Publishers, 1954), 23.

[2] Ibid., 13.

[3] Ibid., 33.

[4] Ibid., 15.

[5] *Figaro,* March 19, 1873.

[6] David Belasco, "My Life Story," *Hearst's Magazine* 25 (May 1914): 649–50.

[7] Arthur H. Fischer, "David Belasco in San Francisco" (M.A. thesis, Stanford University, 1956), 125.

[8] William Winter, *The Life of David Belasco* (New York, 1918), 1:253.

[9] *San Francisco Call,* February 23, 1879.

[10] Fischer, 87.

[11] Winter, 1:97–98.

[12] *Figaro,* February 19, 1877.

[13] *San Francisco Evening Bulletin,* July 16, 1879.

[14] *Argonaut,* July 17, 1979

[15] *San Francisco Call,* March 2, 1884.

'THE PASSION'

[1] Winter, 1:115.

[2] Ibid., 124.

[3] Ibid., 124–25

[4] *San Francisco Theatre Research* 6:2.

[5] *Argonaut,* March 6, 1879.

[6] *Morning Call,* February 23, 1879.

[7] *San Francisco Theatre Research* 6:75.

[8] Fischer, 80.

[9] James O'Neill, "Personal Reminiscences," *Theatre Magazine,* December 1917.

STARS RUSH IN

[1] *San Francisco Evening Bulletin,* June 17, 1884.

[2] McElhaney, 57.

[3] *San Francisco Chronicle,* November 3, 1901.

[4] *San Francisco Chronicle,* May 15, 1889.

[5] Robert Commanday, "The San Francisco Lecouvreur Collection," *San Francisco Chronicle,* September 15, 1985.

[6] *San Francisco Morning Call,* May 24, 1883.

[7] Julia Cooley Altrocchi, *The Spectacular San Franciscans* (New York: Dutton, 1949), 245.

[8] *San Francisco Chronicle*, September 6, 1892.

[9] Mark Twain, *Autobiography* (New York and London: Harper & Brothers, 1924), 1:242.

[10] *San Francisco Call*, March 28, 1882.

[11] *Wasp*, March 31, 1882.

[12] Richard Ellmann, *Oscar Wilde* New York: Vintage Books, 1988), 194.

[13] *San Francisco Chronicle*, May 16, 1887.

[14] Lois Foster Rodecape, "Quand Même: A Few California Footnotes to the Biography of Sarah Bernhardt," *California Historical Society Quarterly* 20, no. 2 (June 1941): 130.

[15] *San Francisco Examiner*, April 26, 1891.

[16] Rodecape, 143.

[17] Altrocchi, 143.

[18] Ibid., 245–46.

[19] *San Francisco Call*, November 11, 1901.

[20] *San Francisco Chronicle*, November 10, 1885.

THE TIVOLI

[1] Robert Commanday, "Tivoli Furor in Early San Francisco," *San Francisco Chronicle*, May 21, 1978.

[2] *San Francisco Chronicle*, August 27, 1899.

[3] Ibid.

[4] John Young, *San Francisco: A History of the Pacific Coast Metropolis* (San Francisco: St. Claire, 1912), 610.

[5] *San Francisco Theatre Research* 8:107.

[6] Ibid.

[7] Alfred Metzger, "A Brief Sketch Concerning the Musical Past," *Pacific Coast Musical Review*, October 1901, 5.

[8] *Argonaut*, January 30, 1905.

[9] *San Francisco Examiner*, March 13, 1913.

[10] *San Francisco Chronicle*, November 18, 1913.

[11] Mabel Porter Pitts, published poem from unidentified source, SF PALM.

[12] George Poultney, "The Old Thespian Mourns the Passing of the Tivoli," *San Francisco Newsletter and Wasp*, January 3, 1950.

[13] Thomas Nunan, "Singers Who Helped Make the Old Tivoli Famous in Early San Francisco Days," *San Francisco Examiner*, October 26, 1924.

THE AGE OF MELODRAMA

[1] Robert C. Toll, *On with the Show: The First Century of Show Business in America* (New York: Oxford University Press, 1976), 148.

[2] *San Francisco News Letter*, December 25, 1886.

[3] *San Francisco Morning Call*, April 13, 1887.

[4] *San Francisco Chronicle*, October 19, 1890.

[5] *San Francisco Theatre Research* 16:291–94.

[6] *San Francisco Call*, July 14, 1895.

[7] *San Francisco Examiner*, May 20, 1898.

[8] *San Francisco Bulletin*, December 25, 1889.

[9] *San Francisco Theatre Research* 16:295.

[10] See A. Nicholas Vardac, *Stage to Screen* (reprint, New York: DaCapo Press, 1987).

SLUMMERS' PARADISE

[1] Lewis, 203–204.

[2] B. E. Lloyd, *Lights and Shades of San Francisco* (San Francisco: Bancroft & Co., 1867), 158.

[3] Herbert Asbury, *The Barbary Coast: An Informal History of the San Francisco Underworld* (Garden City, N.Y.: Garden City Publishing Co., 1933), 131.

[4] Ibid., 135–36.

[5] *San Francisco Examiner*, May 2, 1885.

[6] Gagey, 159.

[7] *San Francisco Chronicle*, April 14, 1889.

[8] Asbury, 123.

[9] Ibid., 287.

[10] Ibid., 286.

AFRICAN AMERICANS TAKE THE STAGE

[1] Tom Stoddard, *Jazz on the Barbary Coast* (Essex, England: Storyville Publications, 1982), 98–103.

[2] Ibid., 100–101.

[3] Ibid., 120.

[4] Ibid.

[5] Russell Hartley, "History of Black Dancers in San Francisco" (unpublished, undated manuscript, SF PALM), 4.

[6] Douglas Henry Daniels, *Pioneer Urbanites: A Social and Cultural History of Black San Francisco* (Philadelphia: Temple University Press, 1990), 125.

[7] *Wasp*, December 2, 1881.

[8] Stoddard, 124.

[9] Marian Hannah Winter, "Juba and American Minstrelsy," *Chronicles of the American Dance*, ed. Paul Magriel (New York: Henry Holt, 1948), 57–58.

[10] Robert C. Toll, *Blacking Up: The Minstrel Show in Nineteenth-Century America* (New York: Oxford University Press, 1974), 201.

[11] *Argonaut*, January 20, 1883.

[12] *Argonaut*, May 6, 1882.

[13] Hartley, 7.

[14] Toll, *On with the Show!*, 122.

[15] Ann Charters, *Nobody: The Story of Bert Williams* (New York: Macmillan, 1970), 27.

[16] Toll, *On with the Show!*, 131.

[17] Ibid., 133.

[18] Toll, *Blacking Up*, 257.

SAN FRANCISCO EMBRACES VAUDEVILLE

[1] Frank Norris, *McTeague* (paperback ed., New York: New American Library, 1981), 79.

[2] Gelett Burgess, *Behind the Scenes: Glimpses of Fin de Siècle*

San Francisco (San Francisco: Grabhorn-Hoyem, 1968), 30.

[3] *San Francisco Chronicle*, July 2, 1882.

[4] McElhaney, 144–45.

[5] Russell Hartley, "History of the Orpheum Theatre" (unpublished, undated manuscript, SF PALM), 3.

[6] *San Francisco Morning Call*, March 24, 1895.

[7] Burgess, 34.

[8] Evelyn Wells, *Champagne Days of San Francisco* (New York: D. Appleton-Century Co., 1939), 30–52.

[9] Dora Barrett and Rose Cordeiro Miller, *My Love Wears Two Masks* (El Cerrito, Calif.: Seaview Press, 1981), 45.

[10] *Wasp*, September 4, 1897.

[11] *San Francisco Chronicle*, December 31, 1896.

[12] *San Francisco Chronicle*, April 1, 1906.

ENTERTAINMENT ALFRESCO

[1] Kevin Starr, *Americans and the California Dream: 1850–1915* (Santa Barbara: Peregrine Smith, 1973), 287.

[2] *San Francisco Theatre Research* 16:32.

[3] Charles Lockwood, "Woodward's Natural Wonders," *California Living* (*San Francisco Chronicle-Examiner*), November 20, 1977, 4.

[4] *Golden Era*, November 11, 1860.

[5] Joanne Lafler, "San Francisco's Bohemian Theatre: 1880–1923," *Encore: Archives for the Performing Arts Quarterly* 2, no. 3 (Summer 1985): 3.

[6] Ibid.

[7] Starr, 381.

[8] *San Francisco Chronicle*, January 8, 1973.

[9] Gray Brechin, "Attic Treasures: Nature, Art and Fredom," *California Monthly*, December 1978, 13.

[10] *San Francisco Chronicle*, January 8, 1973.

[11] Brechin, 13.

WOMEN CHANGE THE DANCE

[1] Gagey, 32.

[2] *San Francisco Theatre Research*, 14:239.

[3] *San Francisco Bulletin*, April 27, 1861.

[4] *San Francisco Bulletin*, January 18, 1867.

[5] *San Francisco Bulletin*, January 11, 1870.

[6] *San Francisco Chronicle*, April 5, 1904.

[7] *San Francisco Chronicle*, February 6, 1905.

[8] *Argonaut*, November 18, 1889.

[9] Margaretta Mitchell, "Dance for Life: Isadora's California Dance Legacy," *Encore: Archives for the Performing Arts Quarterly* 2, no. 4 (Autumn 1985): 4.

[10] Conflicting dates have been published for Duncan's birth. The date given here is based on recent scholarship by dance historians Susan Manning and Ann Daly.

[11] Isadora Duncan, *Isadora Speaks* (San Francisco: City Lights Books, 1981), 25.

[12] Isadora Duncan, *My Life* (3rd printing, New York: Award Books, 1969; originally published New York: Boni and Liveright, 1927), 16–17.

[13] Ibid., 23.

[14] Ibid., 11.

[15] Elizabeth Kendall, *Where She Danced: The Birth of American Art-Dance* (Berkeley, Calif.: University of California Press, 1979), 23–25.

[16] Duncan, *Isadora Speaks*, 24.

[17] Duncan, *My Life*, 20.

[18] Millicent Dillon, *After Egypt: Isadora Duncan and Mary Cassatt* (New York: Dutton, 1990), 164.

[19] Duncan, *Isadora Speaks*, 49.

[20] Duncan, *My Life*, 20.

[21] *San Francisco Call*, February 25, 1903.

[22] *San Francisco Examiner*, February 25, 1903.

[23] *San Francisco Examiner*, July 17, 1910.

[24] Rather, 78.

[25] *San Francisco Examiner*, November 26, 1917.

[26] Lenore Peters Job, *Looking Back While Surging Forward* (San Francisco: Peters Wright, 1984), 67–68.

[27] Duncan, *My Life*, 339.

[28] Dillon, 156.

[29] Agnes de Mille, *The Book of the Dance* (New York: Golden Press, 1963), 137.

[30] Felix Cherniavsky, unpublished article on Maud Allan, SF PALM, December 5, 1892, footnote 15.

[31] Felix Cherniavsky, *The Salome Dancer: The Life and Times of Maud Allan* (Toronto: McCelland and Stewart, 1991), 164.

[32] Ibid., 165.

[33] *San Francisco Chronicle*, April 6, 1910.

[34] *Argonaut*, April 16, 1910.

EARTHQUAKE EVE ON THE TOWN

[1] Oscar Lewis, *Bay Window Bohemia* (Garden City, N.Y.: Doubleday, 1956), 28.

[2] *San Francisco Call*, April 16, 1906.

[3] *San Francisco Theatre Research*, 14:368.

[4] Margot Peters, *The House of Barrymore* (New York: Random House, 1990), 106

[5] *San Francisco Call*, April 17, 1906.

[6] Donald C. Biggs, "Melpomene on the Half Shell," *California Historical Quarterly 33 (no. 1):* 41.

[7] Barrett and Miller, 294.

[8] *San Francisco Call*, April 17, 1906.

[9] Ibid.

[10] Ibid.

[11] Jack London, "The Fire," in *San Francisco Stories: Great Writers on the City*, ed. John Miller (San Francisco: Chronicle Books, 1990), 245.

[12] Peters, 106–107.

[13] Rodecape, 139.

Index

Page numbers in boldface refer to illustrations.

Abott, Bessie, 134
Abbott, Emma, 22
Adams, Maude, 31, **62**, 65
Adrienne Lecouvreur, 45, 50
Africa!, 86, **88**, 89, 114
Ages of Sin, The, 68
Agoust Family, 136
Aladdin's Lamp, 76, 114
Alberta, Mme ("The Black Nightingale"), 86
Alcazar Theater, 42, 53, **64**, 65–67, **68**, 69, 99, 135, 138, 139, **140**
Aldrich, Louis, **65**
Alhambra Theater, 69, 136, **140**. *See also* Bush Street Theater; New Theater
Allan, Maud, 106, 127, 129, **130, 131**
American Theater, 139
Andersons, The, **89**
Anglin, Margaret, 44
Antiope, 112, 115
Are You a Mason?, 135
Aristophanes, 105
Armstrong and Holly, 136
Around the World in Eighty Days, 113, 114
Arthur, Joseph, **66, 67**
Article 47 (play), 69
Assoimoir, L', 33
As You Like It, 106
Azilla "The Flying Dancer," 110
Azurine, 112

B., Betsy, 12, 79
Babes in Toyland, 135
Baby Dody. *See* Barrett, Dora
Baldwin, Lucky, 24, 33, 35
Baldwin's Academy of Music (also called Baldwin's Theater), 15, 21, 22, **23**, 24, 30, 32, 38, 39, 41, 42, 44, 45, 46, 48, 64, 65, 85, 99, 114, **140**
Barrett, Dora, 97
Barrett, Lawrence, 16, 17, 29, 44

Barrie, James, 65
Barrymore, John, Jr., 135, 137
Barrymore, Maurice, **44**
Bauer, Adolph, 94
Bauer, Harold, 124, 125
Bayes, Nora, 97
Beck, Martin, 96
Belasco, David: **31**; as actor: *Gold Demon, The*, 29, 42; *Richard III*, 28; *Romeo and Juliet*, 29; *Uncle Tom's Cabin*, **26**; as writer/producer: *Assoimoir, L'*, 33; *Chums*, 33; *DuBarry*, 39; *Egyptian Mystery, The*, 33; *First Born, The*, 66; *Girl of the Golden West*, 28; *Madame Butterfly*, 39; *Marriage by Moonlight*, 32; *Not Guilty*, 32, 33; *Octoroon, The*, 33, 85; *Olivia*, 32; *Passion, The*, 35–39; *Pawn Ticket No. 210*, 33; *Proof Positive*, 32; *Roll of the Drum*, 27; *Rose of the Rancho*, 28; *Stranglers of Paris*, 63; *Within an Inch of His Life*, 32; *Woman of the People, A*, 32; *Zaza*, 39
Belasco, Fred (brother), 39, 67, 136
Belasco, Walter (brother), 39, 66
Bella Union, **70**, 73–74, 76
Belle Hélène, La, 56
Bellini, Vincenzo: *La Sonnambula*, 20
Belvedere Theater, **140**
Bergere, Valerie, 138
Bernhardt, Sarah, 22, 41; first visit to California, 48–50; **49**, 69, 73, 96, 106, 124, **132, 139**
Bert, Frederick, 22
Bierce, Ambrose, **12**, 19, 45, 46, 47, 48, 103
Bijou Theater, 42, 76
Big Bertha, 74
Birds, The, 105
Bizet, Georges, 33, 134–35
Bland, James, 83
Blind Tom, 89
Bluebeard, 114
Blue Jeans, **66**

Bohemian Club, 48, **100**, 103, **104, 105**
Bonfanti, Marie, 109, 113
Booth, Edwin, 17, 27, 29, 44
Boucicault, Dion, 17, **29**, 30, 33
Bowers, Mrs. D. P., 43
Box, Ted E., 136
Boynton, Florence Treadwell, 118, 125
Brady, Diamond Jim, 46, 137
Brigands, The, 56
British Blondes. *See* Thompson, Lydia
Broadway Theater, **140**
Brougham, John, 17
Brown, Lew, 85
Browne, Bothwell, 114, 136
Buffalo Bill (play), 22. *See also* Cody, Buffalo Bill
Buntline, Ned, 75
Bush Street Theater, 42, 55, 92, 93. *See also* Alhambra Theater; New Theater

California Theater, **13**, 15, 16–20, **21**, 24, 25, 29, 31, **37**, 45, 46, 64, 86, 114, 115, 136, **140**. *See also* New California Theater
Callender's Minstrels, 33, 83–85, **84**
Canal Boat Pinafore, 55
Cantor, Eddie, 97
Carmen, 33, 134, **135**
Carmencita, Mlle., **115**
Caruso, Enrico, 22, 52, 134, **135**, 137
Cavalleria Rusticana, 95
Celeste, Mme. *See* Williams, Celeste
Central Theater, 69, 136, **140**
Chaplin, Charles, 95
Chapman, Blanche, 30
Chapman, Ella, 30, **32**
Cherry and Fair Star, 18, **21**
Cherry Blossom Burlesquers, 136
Cherry Pickers, The, **67**
Chocolate Dandies, 89
Chums, 33
Church, Mrs., 56
Chutes Theater, 89, 97, 135, 136, 137, 138, **140**
Cigale, La, 46
Claxton, Kate, **43**

Cleopatra, 50
Cleveland Genuine Coloured Colossal Carnival Minstrels, 83
Clorindy, **80**, 89
Coghlan, Rose, 32
Cody, Buffalo Bill, 22, **75**, 93.
Cohan, George M., **94**, 95
Collins, Ulric, 138
Colonial Theater, 139, **140**
Columbia Opera Company, 95
Columbia Theater (formerly named Stockwell's), **13**, 65, 89, 99, 114, 125, 135, **140**
Columbus and the Discovery of America, 113
Comique (music hall), 73
Conried, Heinrich, 134
Conway and Leland, **96, 97**
Cook, Will Marion, **80**, 89
Coquelin, Constant, 50, 124
Cornalba, Adele, 110, **111**
Count of Monte Cristo, **37**, 38, 44
Crabtree, Lotta, **11**, 27, 28, **33**, 44, 73, 81, 102
Crawford, Edna A., 136
Creighton, Bertha, 69
Cremorne, Jack. *See* Midway Plaisance
Crystal Slipper, 110

Daly, Augustin, 20, 93, 122
Dame aux Camélias, La, 50
Dan Sang Fung (also called Royal Chinese Theater), 136
Danger Signal, The, 68
Dangers of the Working Girls, 136
Dante Alighieri, **13**
Davenport, Fanny, **18**, 43, **50**
Davies, Phoebe, 65
Davis Theater, **138**
Davy Crockett, 22, 44
DeAngelis, Johnny, 102
Delsarte, François, 118
de Mauprat, Adrien, 18
Dickens, Charles, 46
Dimier, Aurelia, 109
Ditrichstein, Leo, 135
Doll's House, A, 99
Donizetti, Gaetano: *Lucia di Lammermoor*, 52
D'Oyly Carte Opera, 46
Dressler, Marie, 95
DuBarry, 39

Dumas, Alexandre: *Count of Monte Cristo, The,* **37,** 38, 44; *Dame aux Camélias, La,* 50
Dunbar, Paul Laurence: *Clorindy,* **80,** 89
Duncan, Augustin (brother), 121
Duncan, Elizabeth (sister), 121
Duncan, Isadora **108, 109,** 115–127, **117, 120, 123, 124, 126**
Duncan, Raymond (brother), 121, 125
Dupree, Jose, 73

East Lynne, 63
Edouin, Willie, 46
Edwards, Harry, 17
Egyptian Hall, 33
Egyptian Mystery, The, 33
Emerson, Billy, 58, 73, 81, **83**
Emerson, Ralph Waldo, 46
Empire Theater, **140**
Eureka Music Hall, 73
Excelsior, 113, **114**

Famous Criterions, 86
Faust, **52,** 58
Fedora, 48
Fern Hall, 76
Field, Charles K., 104
Fire-Fly, 29
Firefly Social and Dramatic Club, 28, 29
First Born, The, 65
Fischer's Theater, **140**
Fisk University Singers, 82
Fiske, Minnie Maddern, 43, 93
Flag of Truce, A, 68
Florodora, 13
Forrest, Edwin, 17
Foster, Ned, 74
Fountain (variety hall), 76
Four Fleet Sisters, 73
Foy, Eddie, 65, 72
Francesca da Rimini, 13
Fremstad, Olive, 134, 135
Frogs (theatrical organization), 88
Frohman, Charles, 65, 106
Fulford Company, 30
Fuller, Loie, 127, **128**
Funny Mitchells, 89
Furst, W. W., 57, **59**

Garden, Mary, 61
Garrick Theater, 131
Gates, Harry, 60

Georgia Minstrels, 83
Gilbert, John, 74
Gilbert, W. S., 20
Gilbert, W. S. and Arthur Sullivan: *HMS Pinafore,* 55–56, **57,** 73, 102; *Mikado, The,* 56; *Patience,* 46, 56; *Pirates of Penzance,* 56; *Trial by Jury,* 56
Gilded Age, The, 20
Girl of the Golden West, 28
Giselle, 109
Glendenning, Ernest, 135
Gluck, Christoph W., 124
Gold Demon, The, 29–30
Golden Gate Park bandshell, 138
Goldmark, Karl, 134
Goleman's Dogs, Cats, and Doves, 136
Goodwin, Nat C., 65
Gordon, Marie, 17
Gounod, Charles F., **52,** 58
Grace, James, 85
Grais, Herr (animal act), **93**
Grand Opera House, 22, 35, 37, 38, 42, 45, 50, 52, 55, 63, **65,** 68, 69, 85, 109, 114, 134, **140.** *See also* Wade's Opera House
Granger, Maude, 69
Grant, Emma, 85
Grauman, Sid, 138
Great Diamond Robbery, The, 68
Greek Theater, 105–106, **107,** 125, **132,** 139
Greene, Clay M., 20, 33, 63, 86
Green Knight, The, 104
Green Monster, The, 110
Grismer, Joseph R., 65

Hall, Artie, 136
Hamadryads, 105
Hamlet, 44, 45
Hammond Theater, **140**
Harrigan, Edward "Ned," **72,** 93
Hart, Tony, **72**
Harte, Bret, 20, 63, **103**
Harvey, Frank, 65
Haverly's Mastodon Minstrels, 83, 86, 87, 102
Hayes Park, 102
Hayman, Al, 43, 44, 93
Hazel Kirke, 63
Hearts of Tennessee, 138
Henderson, David, 113
Herbert, Victor, 135

Hernani, **49**
Herne, James, 30, 32, 33
Hess, C. D., 95
Hinrichs, Gustav, **60**
HMS Pinafore, 55–56, **57,** 73, 102
Hoffman, Gertrude
Hogan, Ernest, 86
Hooley Minstrels, 92
Houdini, Harry, 95
Howard, Bronson, 20
Hugo, Victor, **49**

Ibsen, Henrik, 99
Ina, 44
In Dahomey, 88, 89
Inferno, **13**
Inman, Pearl, 89
In Old Kentucky, 63, **64**
Iphigenia in Aulis, 124
Irish Princess, An, **64**
Irving, Henry, 22, 41, 45
Irwin, Will, 105
Isadorables, 124
Italian Brigands, 113

Jeanne d'Arc, 50
Jefferson, Joseph, 32
Jesse James, **65**
Job, Lenore Peters, 125
Jolson, Al, 97
Jones, Sissieretta, 89, 95, **99**
Joseph, Erz-Herzog, 95
Judah, Mrs., **16,** 17, **20**
Julius Caesar, 44

Kean, Charles, 28
Kersands, Billy, 85
Kingsley, Walter. *See* Belasco, David
Kipling, Rudyard, 13, 103
Kiralfy Brothers, **112,** 113, **114,** 115
Kreling, Ernestine, 60
Kreling, Joseph, 56, 58, 60
Kremer, Theodore, 136
Kronemanns, The **96**

La Bohème Theater, **140**
Langtry, Lillie, **40,** 41
La Verne, Lucille, 68
Leahy, William "Doc," 60
Leavitt, Michael, 43, 76, 92, 93
Lecocq, Alexandre, 57
Lehman family, 110
Lewis, Sam, 85
Life's Revenge, A, 29
Little Egypt, 74, **77**
Locke, Charles, 92
London Assurance, 17

Lost in London, 74
Love, 20
Lucia di Lammermoor, 52
Lucky Coon, A, 88
Lyster, F. W., 20, 32
Lytell, Bertram, 65

Macbeth, 18
McCullough, "Genial"
John, **19**, 24, 25, **28**;
and the California
Theater, 16–20, **21**, 29,
45
Macdonough Theater, 138
Mackaye, Steele, 63
Madame Butterfly, 39
Magic Trumpet, The, 110
Maguire, Thomas, 18, 19,
22, 24, 25, 30, 31; Pas-
sion, The, 35–39, **36**,
39; 46, 92
Maguire's New Theater, 29
Maguire's Opera House, 18,
24, 27
Maguire's Unequalled Com-
pany, 31
Majestic Theater, 135, 138,
140
Man in the Forest, The, 104
Manon, 52
Mansfield, Richard, 44
Mantelli, Eugenia, 52
Mapleson, Col. John Henry,
50, 52, 53
Market Street Theater, 56,
76
Marlowe, Julia, 23
Marriage by Moonlight, 32
Marseillaise, La, 124, 125
Martinetti, Ignacio, 135
Martinetti troupe, 102, 110,
113
Mascagni, Pietro, **60**, 95
Massenet, Jules, 52, **53**
Mayall, Herschel, 69
Maybeck, Bernard, 119
Mayer, Milton, 67
Mayo, Frank, 44, 93
Mazeppa, 55, 74
Melba, Nellie, 22, 41, **52**
Melville, Emelie, **17**, 55,
57, 60
Mendelssohn, Jakob, 129,
130, **131**
Menken, Adah Isaacs, 74
Merchant of Venice, The, 44
Merola, Gaetano, 52
Metropolitan Theater, 18,
27, 29, 30
Meyer, Milton, 136
Midsummer Night's

Dream, A, 106, **120**, 122
Midway Plaisance (origi-
nally Jack Cremorne's),
74, 87
Mikado, The, 56
Mikado on the Half Shell,
136
Miss Timidity, 135
Mission Theater, **140**
M'Liss, or The Child of the
Sierras, 20, 63
Modjeska, Helena, 23, **45**
Monplaisir Dance Troupe,
109
Monro, Randolph, 119
Montezuma, 104
Morgan, Julia, 105
Morosco, Walter, 22, 67–69
Morosco's Opera House. See
Wade's Opera House;
Grand Opera House
Morris, Clara, 43, **48**
Morse, Salmi, 35, 38
Mother Earth, 66
Mother Goose, 114
Motoring, 135
Mozart Hall, 82
Musette, 44
My Life (Duncan), 109, 116,
121
My Life and Dancing
(Allan), 130
My Partner, **65**

Neilson, Adelaide, **16**, 17,
20, **28**, 29, 32
Nevada, Emma, 53, 64
New Alhambra Theater, 24
New Bush Theater, 83
New California Theater, 25,
42, 44, 99. See also Cali-
fornia Theater
New National Theater, 138
New Pantages, 98. See also
Orpheum Theater
New Theater, 82, 92. See
also Bush Street
Theater
Nielsen, Alice, 60
Nobles, Milton, 65
Norton, "Emperor" Joshua,
29
Norton the First, 29
Not Guilty, 32, 33
Novelty Theater, 139, **140**

Oates, Alice, 55
Oberon Theater, **140**
Octoroon, The, 33, 85
Offenbach, Jacques, 56
Old Liberty Playhouse, Ye,
138

Olivia, 32
O'Neil, Nance, 65, **69**
O'Neill, James, 31, 32, **34**,
35–38, **37**, **38**, 44
Oofty Goofty, 74
Operator, The, 68
Orpheum Theater (also
called Orpheum Opera
House), 85, 86, 89, **90**,
91–99, **96**–**97**, **135**,
138, 139, **140**
Otello (Verdi), 58
Othello (Shakespeare), 44

Pace that Kills, The, 68
Palace Hotel, 20–21, **25**
Papinta, **95**
Parepa-Rosa, Euphrosyne,
109
Paris, Mlle, 115
Paris, or the Apple of Dis-
cord, 19
Park Theater, 138
Partington, Blanche, 12, 52,
135
Passion, The, 33–39, **34**
Pastor, Tony, 46, 55
Pathétique Symphony, 124
Patience, 46, 56
Patti, Adelina, 41, 50, **51**
Pawn Ticket No. 210, 33
Perkins, Walter, 135
Phèdre, **139**
Phillips, Watts, 32, 33
Pinero, Arthur Wing, 64
Pirates of Penzance, 56
Plaisted, Gracie, 60
Platt's Hall, 46
Porter, W. T., 17
Potter, Mrs. James Brown,
41
Powers, Francis, 65, 66
Pride, Sam, 83
Primrose and West
Vaudeville Troupe, 89
Proof Positive, 32
Puccini, Giacomo: Tosca,
La, 50
Pygmalion and Galatea, 20

Qualitz, Clara, 110
Quarrelsome Neighbors,
136
Queen of the Highbinders,
136
Queen of Sheba, The, 134

Racine, Jean, **139**
Ralston, Billy, **14**, 16, 17,
20, 21, 24, 25
Raoul, or the Magic Star,
110

Ravel, Gabriel, 110
Raymond, John, 17
Ready! or California in '71, 20
Redding, Joseph D., 104
Red Gnome, The, 110
Red Onion Opera House, 81
Red Spider, The, 68
Reed, Charlie, 58
Rehan, Ada, 43, **48**
Richard III, 18, 24, 28
Richelieu, 18
Rip Van Winkle, 17, 22
Rivals, The, 18
Riviere (impersonator), 95
Roberts, Theodore, 68
Robertson, Peter, 12, 103, 104
Robinson, Bill "Bojangles," 89
Robinson, Yankee, 102
Roll of the Drum, 27
Romeo and Juliet, **16, 20,** 29, 74
Rose of the Rancho, 28
Rosner's Electric Orchestra, 94
Rousset Sisters, 109
Royal Chinese Theater. *See* Dan Sang Fung
Russell, Lillian, **46**, 95

Saint Patrick at Tara, 104
Salvini, Tommaso, 45
Sanderson, Sybil, 22, 52, **53**
San Francisco Minstrels, 81
Sangalli, La Rita, 109, 113
Santley, Mabel, 76, 92
Saratoga, 20
Sardou, Victorien, 48
Scouts of the Plains, 75
Seig, Martin, 86
Seneca, Lucius Annaeus: *Trojan Women, The*, 106
Shakespeare, William, 13, 17; *As You Like It*, 106; *Julius Caesar*, 44; *Macbeth*, 18; *Merchant of Venice, The*, 44; *Midsummer Night's Dream, A*, 106, **120,** 122; *Richard III*, 18, 24, 28; *Romeo and Juliet*, **16, 20,** 29, 74
Shaw, George Bernard, 64
She, 57, **59**
Sheridan, Richard, 18
Sinbad the Sailor, 19, 76, 114
Skinner, Otis, 23, **44**
Smith, W. H. Sedley, 20

Sonnambula, La, 20
Snowflake, 22
South San Francisco Opera House, 136
Spanish Kitty, 73
Sparks, Edouin, 93
Spring Song, 129, **130, 131**
Standard Theater, 55, **57,** 76
Stevens, Ashton, 12, 134, 139
Stevenson, Robert Louis, 103
Stockmeyer family, 60
Stockwell, Lincoln, 65
Stockwell's Theater. *See* Columbia Theater
Stowe, Harriet Beecher, **26,** 29, 64, **85**
Stranglers of Paris, 63
Strassburg Music Hall, 73
Strauss, Johann, 56
Sullivan, Barry, 24, **42,** 44
Swain, Carrie, 93
Sweet, Charles R., 135
Sylphide, La, 109, 110

Tchaikovsky, Pëtr Ilich, 124
Temple of the Wings, 118, **119**
Terry, Ellen, 22, 45
Tetlow, Samuel, 74
Tetrazzini, Luisa, 52, **60**
Thais, 53
Theatrical Syndicate, 13, 23, 43, 50, 65, 93, 99
Theodora, 50
Thompson, Charlotte, 17
Thompson, Lydia, 18, **73,** 76, 110
Tivoli Opera House, 42, **54,** 55–61, **58, 59,** 65, 135, **138, 140**
Tosca, La, 50
Treadwell, Florence. *See* Boynton, Florence Treadwell
Trial by Jury, 56
Trip to Turkey!, A, 86
Trip to the Moon, A, 113
Trojan Women, The, 106
Trollope, Anthony, 46
Trovatore, Il, 61
Tucker's Academy of Music, 29
Tucker, Sophie, 97
Twain, Mark, 20, 46, 103

Uncle Tom's Cabin, **26,** 29, 64, **85**
Under the Gaslight, 20
Union Hall, 67, 68, 76

Unique Theater, 138, **140**

Vaidis Sisters, **97**
Valerga family, 60, **61**
Van Ness Theater, 139
Verne, Jules, 113, 114
Verdi, Giuseppe: *Otello*, 58; *Trovatore, Il*, 61
Vigna, Arturo, 134
Vision of Salome, The, 127, 129–30
Von Suppe, Franz, 57

Wade's Opera House, 15, 21, 22, 24. *See also* Grand Opera House
Wagner, Richard, 129
Waldron, Charles, 135
Walker, Ada Overton, 88
Walker, George, **78,** 79, 86–89, **87**
Wall, Jimmy, 136
Wallack, Lester, 32
Wallenrod, George, 64, 66
Walter, Gustav, **92,** 93–96
Way Down East, 22
Weber and Fields, 95
Whitman, Walt, 46
Who Goes There?, 135
Wife's Peril, A, 41
Wigwam Variety Hall, 76, 93
Wilde, Oscar, 41, 46, **47,** 65, 103, 129
Williams, Mme Celeste, 109, **110**
Williams, Bert, **4, 78,** 79, 86–89, **87**
Willows, The, 101
Wills, Nat, **98**
Winter Garden, 57
Within an Inch of His Life, 32
Woman Against Woman, 65
Woman of the People, A, 32
Woodward's Gardens, **102**
Wreck of the Pinafore, The, 56
Wrong Count Tobacco, The, 136

Zavistowski Sisters, 110
Zaza, 39
Ziegfeld Follies, 88, 89
Zola, Emile, 33
Zoulouw, Millia, 82

Index compiled by Lena Strayhorn

The San Francisco Performing Arts Library & Museum (SF PALM) is a nonprofit institution dedicated to collecting, preserving, and making available materials on the performing arts. The collection, the largest of its kind on the West Coast, includes both national and international holdings, but focuses principally on the rich heritage of the lively arts in the San Francisco Bay Area—from the rough-and-tumble Gold Rush, through the Great Earthquake, to the current wealth of world-class music, dance, and theater.

Located in the heart of San Francisco's performing arts center, the Performing Arts Library & Museum features more than one million historic programs, photographs, playbills, and press clippings, as well as a core collection of scene and costume designs, fine art, artifacts, videotapes, periodicals, and books, including one of the largest collections of dance materials in the West.

The collection concentrates on those performing arts presented in a live, theatrical venue—music, dance, opera, theater—and documents companies both large and small, art both experimental and mainstream, individual artists as well as major institutions. The multicultural art forms that have long contributed to the diversity of Bay Area culture are also represented in the Library's holdings. The collection is available to the public on a non-circulating basis, for the purposes of research, education, and enjoyment.

The Performing Arts Library & Museum—founded by the late Russell Hartley—is privately funded and depends upon the contributions of its supporters and dues of its members. Membership is open to all. Thanks to its members and supporters, the Library & Museum presents a lively series of publications, exhibitions, and lectures throughout the year.

Through these and other services, the San Francisco Performing Arts Library & Museum hopes to encourage study in all aspects of our performing arts heritage, to foster the exchange of ideas and resources, and, most importantly, to preserve and protect irreplaceable traces of our past as a foundation for future greatness.